Hunting Ghosts

A Paranormal

Investigator's Guide

Russell Vogels

DEDICATION

To all the past and present paranormal investigators around the world who have, even in the face of skepticism, derision, and sometimes outright hostility continued on their own personal quest to prove the seemingly unprovable. Your accumulated actions, research, and knowledge form the very foundation by which future investigators can build on. Never give up and never give in to the closed minded naysayers and non-believers, for one day, you will be vindicated.

"There are three classes of people: those who see, those who see when they are shown, and those who do not see." — LEONARDO DA VINCI

About the Author

Russ Vogels has been investigating and researching the Paranormal extensively over the past 40 years. His initial introduction to the Paranormal began at age 12 when his family first moved into a highly active home; originally a hotel built in the late 1920's, where phantom footsteps, shadowy apparitions, and doors opening and closing became almost an everyday occurrence. That early exposure sparked a lifelong interest in seeking to explain the seemingly unexplainable. As a professional Security Management Consultant, Legal Investigator, and Forensics Specialist; Russ utilizes his extensive education, training, and experience in his never ending quest to seek answers to the paranormal world around us. Russ's approach to ghost hunting will hopefully get you to engage your brain, sharpen your observational skills, and in the end get you to think like a true investigator would.

Table of Contents

This picture was taken on September 19, 1936 at
Raynham Hall in Norfolk, England. She is believed to be
Lady Dorothy Walpole, sister to Sir Robert Walpole
(England's first Prime Minister). Born in 1686 and is said to
have died of smallpox in 1726. Two additional rumors have
it that she was died from a broken neck after she was
pushed down the grand staircase or that she was
imprisoned at Raynham Hall by her husband after she had
an affair. The first reported occurrence was in the early
1800s and has been seen repeatedly since then. Photo
has been analyzed by experts for over 77 years and, to
date, no one has proven that the picture is a hoax.

Introduction

Welcome to the always interesting and sometimes scary world of ghost hunting. **Hunting Ghosts: A Paranormal Investigator's Guide** is written for the beginning or novice level investigator to give you a general overview and basic understanding of paranormal investigation and the spirit/ghostly realm; along with a fundamental outline of how to properly "ghost hunt". The goal here is not to make you an overnight "instant expert" in all things pertaining to ghost hunting, no one can do that, but simply to give you the needed knowledge and tools necessary to get you started out right; and above all else, to make you think.

Keep in mind that paranormal investigation in general, by its very nature and subject matter, does not operate in or conform to any rigid set of hierarchical scientific rules. In other words, there are no scientific absolutes when it comes to ghost hunting. All that's really required here is an open, but healthily skeptical, mind to begin. Your first and foremost order of business is to "master the basics". Once you do that, you'll have a solid base to build on.

Then, with experience and a little more knowledge, you'll quickly find yourself being looked to as a very competent, if not expert, ghost hunter.

Remember, "Mastering the Basics" is the first and most necessary step, not just in Paranormal Investigation, but in really anything you do in life. When I speak of mastering the basics though, I'm not referring to the simplistic rote regurgitation of facts you would find in a classroom setting, that's easy. What I'm referring to is developing your ability to actually think and analyze, and be able to find and implement alternative means and methods to finding solutions to the questions and problems at hand. Once you've reached that point, everything falls into place and there will be no stopping you. Realize that a paranormal investigation is fluid and ever changing, and as such, requires you to be adaptable, quick thinking, and open minded.

Good luck, have fun, and always be safe.

This photo was taken in 1966 by Rev. Ralph Hardy in the Queen's House section of the National Maritime Museum in Greenwich, England. Hardy, a retired clergyman, intended only to take a picture of the impressive Tulip Staircase but also captured this apparition of a robed figure ascending the stairs. The original negative was examined by experts, including some from Kodak, who deemed that the photo had not been tampered with. People have reported seeing unexplained figures and the sound of footsteps in the same vicinity for years prior to and after this picture was taken.

My Story Begins

My introduction to the paranormal and ghostly hauntings really began at age 12. At that time our family lived in an old (late 1920s) two-story house that was originally built and used as a hotel. It was an every-day and every-night occurrence to hear phantom footsteps going up and down the stairways and hallways, see doorknobs turning, toilet flushing, and doors opening and closing on their own. Everyone in the house experienced the phenomenon on a fairly regular basis to the point where it was accepted as no big deal. For the most part, it was simply disconcerting and at times annoying.

One of the most active areas in the house was the second floor, where my bedroom was located and where I first saw the "shadow person" who appeared numerous times over the course of about five years or so. That was actually the only time I was ever frightened (definite understatement) of anything in the house. Truthfully, so traumatic and creepy was that initial experience, 47 years later, I still sleep with a light on.

One of the most bizarre paranormal events I can remember as a teenager occurred when I was a senior in high school. Growing up in the rural Missouri Ozarks in the late 60s and early 70s meant that you had to seek out things to keep you entertained and one of those things, for us, meant searching for and exploring many of the old and abandoned (haunted?) houses scattered around the countryside. One Friday evening several of us decided to drive out to an old abandoned farmstead about 10 miles out of town, down a long and winding dirt road, that was claimed to be haunted.

As we pulled up, we observed what appeared to be a late 1800s or very early 1900s two-story farmhouse, obviously abandoned years prior, with a straight clear stone walkway leading from the front gate to the front porch of the house. We got out our flashlights and walked straight down the walk to the house. The door was wide open so we went inside and proceeded to explore. While we're on the first floor we heard noises and what we perceived as footsteps and muffled voices coming from the upstairs. After going upstairs we heard the same thing, but coming from downstairs. Our interest now peaked, but pressed for time, we decided to come back at a later date and explore further.

A couple of weeks later we got a chance to go back. Upon arriving at the house again we immediately felt something was very different, as if the place had aged another 100 years overnight. As we walked through the front gate and down, what two weeks earlier was a straight clear stone walkway, our path was blocked by a huge oak tree, two feet in diameter, growing in the middle of the walkway. Two weeks before, the closest tree of any kind, was at least 50 feet from the walkway in all directions. The atmosphere around the house had also changed. It felt heavy, oppressive, and what I would now characterize as malevolent. Had we stepped into or out of some type of dimensional or time shift? Had something placed that tree there, as a warning not to return? I don't know. Something said leave, so we did.

Fast forward, to another strange incident that actually happened to me not too long ago. I had just finished watching a mini marathon of paranormal TV (yes, I watch all the paranormal shows – they're great entertainment) when I noticed my cell phone was beeping to tell me I had a voicemail. That in itself was a little bit unusual since my phone was next to me and had not rung all evening. I checked the calling number and it said 0000000000. The message was this guttural demonic sounding someone or something speaking in what sounded maybe like some dead language (Aramaic?). It scared the crap out of me and at the same time pissed me off. That's not the end of it though. Three different times over the next week I was attacked in bed by some malevolent dark form. Through a combination of protection and banishment techniques, I got rid of the problem. Why it happened, I have no clue. What it was, I think I know but can't prove.

That tends to be one of the drawbacks in conducting investigations and generally playing around in the paranormal realm if you're not careful; you may carry a spirit home with you or they may in fact seek you out just to mess with you. My attitude about spirits in my home is this; come with good or even neutral intentions and I'll simply ask you to leave if you become annoying, come with bad intentions and I'll do my best to banish your butt back to whatever dark hole you crawled out of, guaranteed.

And if I can't do it, I can find a hundred people that can.

Let me be real clear - Your home is supposed to be your castle and you should feel safe there at all times. That's one of the reasons why I never recommend anyone ever doing séances, using a Ouija board, or anything else that would call spirits in to a normally *ghost free* home. There are so many other places to investigate and be creeped out by, so keep it away from your home if at all possible.

Over the past 40+ years I've experienced literally countless unexplainable paranormal events ranging from rapping and footsteps to full-blown apparitions, and everything in between. Some I have been fortunate to document, most have just been my own. More than likely, as you delve further into investigating the paranormal, the vast amount of experiences you'll have will also be your own, and no one else's. Having your own undocumented experiences doesn't make the event less true; as long as you have done due diligence in trying to explain it from a more rational and less paranormal perspective first (debunking).

Remember, not all things that go bump in the night, or for that matter daytime, are the result of a ghostly haunting - but then again.....?

This picture was taken in 1959 by Mable Chinnery while visiting her mother's gravesite. According to Mable, her husband was the only person in the car at the time. When she developed the film, she noticed someone in the backseat – her dead mother. Analyzed by photographic experts and has never been debunked.

The State of Ghost Hunting

The quest to answer the question of whether ghosts exist has been with us for eons. Popularity of all things paranormal has ebbed and flowed over time starting in the mid 1800's and peaking in the early 1920s with the Spiritualist Movement, and then slowly declining through the next 50 years or so before literally exploding again to what it is today. Much of today's popularity, at least in my opinion, can be directly correlated to the advent of the World Wide Web. Instant communication was now possible across the globe, knowledge and results could be shared and compared, fostering even further interest and participation from an ever widening audience.

Add to that a plethora of very entertaining television shows, social media, instant publishing capability, advances in audio and video, better environmental detection technology, and an explosion in haunted tourism that welcomes the errant chill seeker to visit or even stay at supposedly haunted locations all around the world. Now anyone with a desire to ghost hunt can, and the great thing is that it's accepted and not thought of as some heretical activity, at least by vast majority of people.

An individual's decision and motivation to get involved in ghost hunting is probably as varied as asking someone why they decided to be a doctor or why they collect stamps. As far as paranormal investigation goes, I believe it has to do with two primary reasons that are unique to paranormal investigation itself; the creepy/scared factor combined with the inherent quest to answer that age-old question of what happens after you die. Combine that with; it's relatively inexpensive to get started, it has no real age or physical restrictions, and it's a heck of a lot of fun and exciting to do; means that it's ripe for mass participation and enjoyment. As to whether ghost hunting and paranormal investigation in general will ever lose its popularity and appeal like it did in the 1920's, I don't think so. The sheer scope of current participation has reached a point where it's now almost self-perpetuating.

Photograph was taken at Combermere Abbey Library in 1891 by Sybell Corbet. The exposure length was approximately one hour. The figure of a man, said to be Lord Combermere, appears to be sitting in the armchair. At the time this photograph was being taken, Lord Combermere (a top British cavalry commander) was being buried four miles away.

Scientific Investigation or Pseudoscience?

The paranormal research community and the traditional scientific community have been at odds with each other forever it seems, not only from the scientific methodology standpoint, but from the traditionalist's contention that since standard scientific methods can't prove the existence of ghosts or spirits, they simply don't exist. So the question remains; is it science or pseudoscience?

The Oxford English Dictionary defines the scientific method as: "a method or procedure that has characterized natural science since the 17th century, consisting in systematic observation, measurement, and experiment, and the formulation, testing, and modification of hypotheses". From that, we can formulate a theory which offers insight into the physical world, obtained by this empirical research and testing, that is then generally accepted as being an accurate explanation of the phenomena.

Pseudoscience on the other hand is generally defined as: "a claim, belief, or practice which is presented as scientific, but does not adhere to a valid scientific method, lacks supporting evidence or plausibility, cannot be reliably tested, or otherwise lacks scientific status, is often characterized by the use of vague, contradictory, exaggerated or un-provable claims, an over-reliance on confirmation rather than rigorous attempts refutation, a lack of openness to evaluation by other experts, and a general absence of systematic processes to rationally develop theories". Obviously written by a traditionalist..........!

In my opinion we're actually comparing apples and oranges. The standard "scientific method" is really designed for the measurable "physical world", not the paranormal one. Not everything in this world can be quantified or qualified (as of yet) according to some predefined checklist, as some would lead you to believe. Don't let the close minded naysayers and skeptics get in your way. Remember historically, those same type people who disparage the paranormal researchers of today, for the longest time once believed the earth was flat and the sun revolved around the earth. Oh, how times change and new revelations come to pass as our knowledge increases.

Paranormal investigation is, and probably always will be considered pseudoscience, because of one simple fact; your findings cannot be duplicated in the traditional sense. Yes, you can use scientific methods and scientific tools to help gather evidence but in the end you're still dealing with un-duplicable anomalies, no matter how convincing they may seem. Truthfully, at this moment in time, it just doesn't matter that much. Contrary to what the traditional scientific community says..... Ghosts are real! Whether we can ever conclusively prove that, to their satisfaction... maybe, maybe not... only time will tell.

Photograph was taken in 1988 in New York City by a professional fire department accident investigator just prior to extricating the driver from the car wreck. Misty image is believed to be an "Angel" spirit – rushing to the aid of the driver who miraculously survived the ordeal. Photograph and negative have been tested by experts and they can find no evidence of a hoax.

A word of Caution is in order.....

Ghost hunting can be fun and personally rewarding, but it can't be stressed enough, for your safety, to thoroughly check out a location in daylight and to always remember to listen to that little voice inside you. My story of the tree in the walkway is a good example. If that little voice, or sixth sense inside you starts telling you to stop, backup, walk away, or run like hell – do it.

I'm reminded of a line from a poem that says; "For fools rush in where angels fear to tread". Don't be a fool. If it looks and feels unsafe, don't proceed. If the "creepiness meter" is off the charts, don't proceed. I know too many people who have blindly walked into locations at night and have fallen through floors, been exposed to toxic substances, stepped into holes, and had objects fall on them; all because they acted the fool and didn't do the proper prep work.

The same holds true if you were to encounter some type of malevolent entity. Challenging and inviting any type of malicious or malevolent entity to attack you in any way may make for good TV, but only a fool would do it. Just ask all the people who've been physically and psychically attacked or had their lives completely disrupted by some malevolent entity following them home.

One of the most underestimated dangers that investigators can face is of the human kind. This is especially true when investigating at night in both rural and urban settings. Much too often you'll find the supposedly abandoned building you're intent on investigating occupied by squatters, meth cookers, thugs, or general degenerates who don't appreciate your intrusion and can pose a real danger to you and any team members. My suggestion, if possible, is to back off and let the property owner and police deal with the situation if anything like that ever arises. As to whether you choose to carry some type of personal protection device while investigating, that's up to you alone to decide.

Again, don't be a statistic. Use your brain and common sense.

This infra-red photograph was taken during a paranormal investigation at a Toys R' Us in Sunnyvale, California. The man leaning against the shelves in the background was not seen with the naked eye. Other shots taken at the same time with high speed film showed no trace of him.

Ghosts by Any Other Name

The concept of ghosts, real or imagined, has literally been with us since the beginning of time; in every culture, country, region, and religion. A good general definition of a ghost is: the soul or spirit of a dead person or animal that can appear in visible form or through other manifestations to the living; and generally haunt particular locations, objects, or people they were associated with in life. There are literally dozens and dozens of descriptive words for ghost such as; apparition, bogey, familiar spirit, haint, haunt, materialization, phantasm, phantom, poltergeist, shade, shadow, specter, spirit, spook, sprite, vision, visitant, or wraith to name a few.

Whatever the particular word used; the definition of the manifestation of a soul or spirit of a dead person or animal will hold true as a general rule in most cases. You will run across some individuals in the paranormal field who have disdain for any type of general definition and will go out of their way to make sure everyone around knows what the "precise" definition is, which is fine. Ignore it and go on. Life is too short to argue about silly things. Look at it in this context; an apparition is a ghost but all ghosts don't manifest as apparitions…etc..etc. I saw a ghost, you saw an apparition…. and you know what…. we're both right.

At the end of the book I have included a glossary of many paranormal terms for those of you who refuse to be imprecise.

Intelligent Hauntings
An intelligent haunting, in the traditional sense, is where the ghost or entity is aware of, interacts with, responds to, and is able to communicate with the living. Generally most intelligent hauntings are considered to be that of the ghost or spirit of a person who was once among the living. There are a number of thoughts as to why a particular ghost or spirit may be in residence at a particular location, including:

(1) Overriding emotional attachment or connection with a person, place, or thing.
(2) Uncompleted or unfinished earthly business.
(3) They don't realize or acknowledge that they have actually died.
(4) The need to rectify an injustice done to them or others.

(5) The fear of being judged in death.

(6) The need to deliver a message to or watch over friends and loved ones.

(7) Assisting someone who is dying and passing over.

(8) Lonely and seeking company with the living or other spirits who may also be present.

(9) Traumatic death or reliving traumatic events.

(10) Just passing through.

Typically, the intelligent haunting will make its presence known by way of a myriad of different manifestations including: hiding and moving objects, opening and closing doors, turning on and off such things as lights or faucets, disturbance of electrical devices and monitors, footsteps and tapping, disembodied voices, cold spots, battery drain, light anomalies, apparitions, or even physical touching.

Good or Bad in Life – Same in Death

It's important to note again that most intelligent hauntings are considered to be that of the ghost or spirit of a person who was once among the living. Who and what that person was in life will not likely change in death. If the person was a happy, loving, caring, and positive individual in life; they will most likely be that in death. Conversely, if they were angry and hateful in life; death will not change that either. The death of the physical body does not change the core essence or soul of the individual, that's up to choice.

Contrary to what some think, traditional intelligent hauntings are not evil, though they could take on what would be classified as malevolent characteristics due to their own personality traits, or maybe something as simple as not being happy with being disturbed or harassed by a continuing parade of paranormal investigators who are disrespectful and think provocation is okay. With that said; do everybody a favor and treat the ghost or spirit in the same manner that you would treat a living human being or for that matter you yourself would want to be treated.

A number of paranormal investigators and writers have claimed that the traditional intelligent haunting is a rarity. From my own experience and knowledge, I find the opposite to be true, in cases where a conclusive determination of ghost activity actually could be made. Many times investigators will, in the absence of any real evidence of an intelligent haunting, relegate their findings, or lack of findings, to something else entirely, such as a residual haunting, instead of simply saying; "our findings are inconclusive" or "we found nothing to substantiate the claims" at this time. Whether you determine the haunting is intelligent, residual, or something else; say-so and don't be wishy-washy about your findings, or lack thereof.

Residual Hauntings

A residual haunting is probably best described as a lasting energy imprint that can replay itself again and again, much as you would from an audio or video recorder. Residual hauntings, unlike intelligent hauntings, are not interactive. Whether sight, sound, or smell; the same manifestation occurs normally in the same place, at the same time, and under the same circumstances - like a broken record, with absolutely no acknowledgment or interaction between what is being heard, seen, smelled, or felt; and the individual or investigator experiencing the manifestation.

To attempt to explain residual hauntings, most paranormal researchers will point to something called the Stone Tape Theory which was proposed around 1970 as one explanation for ghosts. The idea behind the theory was actually postulated by numerous investigators for decades previous to that. The theory itself speculates that inanimate materials can absorb some form of energy from living beings and that this recording happens especially during moments of high tension, such as a murder, or during intense moments of someone's life. This stored energy then can be released, resulting in a display of the recorded activity similar to a movie or sound loop.

Technically, a residual haunting is not a ghostly or spirit haunting in the strictest sense. There is no ghost or spirit present, only a recorded imprint. Consider the residual hauntings that occur frequently at past high energy locations, such as Civil War battlefields, where cannon and small arms fire can be heard and recorded some 150 years or more after the battle. Residual hauntings are also prevalent in other past high energy sites such as; hospitals, insane asylums, prisons, and accident locations. Tragedy, pain, and suffering can leave, it seems, a profound psychic imprint on the surrounding area.

A question that puzzles even the most diehard believer when thinking about residual hauntings are; "Even if I believe the energy imprint theory to be true, why doesn't the energy dissipate over time and cease to occur?" The answer is that there are actually many incidences of past residual hauntings that occurred for decades and then simply and abruptly stopped. The reason for this is unknown. It could possibly have to do with the belief that certain areas, especially those containing such things as moving water and limestone formations, tend to act as some sort of earth battery to recharge, magnify, and hold a residual haunting. If that earth battery is somehow missing or disturbed, energy dissipation would most likely be the consequence.

Other possibilities may be solar flares, general disturbances or changes in the earth's magnetic field, or even introduction of manmade electromagnetic fields from power lines. Actually, no one has any type of definitive answer at this time; just like a lot of things in the paranormal realm, "they're yet to be discovered".

Demonic Hauntings

Generally a demonic haunting is attributed to an intelligent evil entity of inhuman origin. Throughout recorded history, virtually all cultures have named and described various evil inhuman entities, blaming them for everything from poor harvests to birth defects. Today the term "demonic" is generally associated with the devil (Satan), Christian religion in general, and the Catholic Church in particular. As to whether a demonic haunting is of a satanic origin, the result of some type of universal negative energy buildup or something yet to be discovered is up for debate. The thing that is not debatable among paranormal investigators, as a whole, is that this type of entity is "evil" by all definitions.

A demonic haunting is by definition also an intelligent haunting. Many paranormal investigators may misclassify a standard intelligent haunting as a demonic haunting and vice versa depending on the level of interaction and degree of perceived malevolent activity that has taken or is taking place. There are a number of signs that have been observed over the years that may indicate you're dealing with a demonic haunting such as:

* There is the presence of strong unpleasant smells and foul odors.
* Manifestations are at first very pleasant and nonthreatening but quickly turn nasty and threatening.
* Apparitions appear as human with either no or reddish glowing eyes.
* People have received scratches to their bodies (many times in series of three which is thought to be mocking of the Holy Trinity).
* Objects may move in a reverse or counterclockwise motion.
* Activity occurs in patterns of three (again, mocking of the Holy Trinity)
* Victims report anger and hatred toward others, fear, sorrow, or deep depression that is totally unusual and out of character.
* Victims may come down with sudden mysterious illnesses that defy diagnosis or medical treatment.
* Low guttural growling is heard.
* Activity often peaks at around 3 AM (mocking of the Holy Trinity and referring to the anti-hour since Christ is thought to have been crucified at around three o'clock in the afternoon).
* Suspected Possession (time to call in the experts!).

As to why a demonic entity has chosen to make itself known at that particular location is not fully known. Some believe that there may be some type of natural entrance or portal, if you wish, to the underworld; others believe these demonic entities are summoned, both inadvertently and purposefully, by way of séances, Ouija boards, black magic, and the like. I'm actually a believer in both theories.

The demonic entity is a deceiver, posing initially most often as a completely benign nonthreatening spirit, such as a small child or a departed relative. This is to attempt to gain the victims trust. Its goal is actually to manipulate and harm. It is said with time the demon will eventually reveal its true nature. Dealing with this type of haunting is as dangerous as it gets. Do not provoke or try and take this entity on by yourself. For a true demonic haunting you need to call in an expert demonologist or priest who has the experience and wherewithal to deal with it correctly.

Portal Hauntings
Portals are generally thought to be openings or doorways by which spirits or other entities may freely

and easily pass between the physical and spirit worlds. The concept of portal hauntings is actually not something new. Throughout history many cultures and civilizations, including the Native Americans, have built monuments, religious sites, and burial grounds on what were deemed to be spots where the spirits of the dearly departed could easily transition between this world and the next. Given that rationale, it only makes sense that this transitional doorway opens both ways.

While portals can exist virtually anywhere, there does seem to be some correlation between many of the old cemeteries and ancient burial grounds, along with underground waterways, and Ley lines. That's not to infer that all old cemeteries and the like are portal locations, quite the contrary, but there is enough circumstantial evidence to indicate these very old locations have a higher incidence and propensity for what would be deemed a portal type haunting. Typically the activity found at a portal site varies. It may include orbs and other light anomalies, apparitions of humans or odd creatures, mists, disembodied voices, or even demonic type entities.

What sets a portal type haunting apart is usually the sheer number and amount of activity present.

The actual existence of portals is a debatable subject among many investigators. Most, I would say, would come down on the side of their probable existence, though like most things in the paranormal world, that belief has yet to be conclusively proved to anyone's satisfaction. My own personal opinion is that they do exist. As to why, I'm not sure but I think it may have to do with some type of naturally occurring electromagnetic junction similar to that proposed by, and just as hotly contested in, British archaeologist Alfred Watkins' 1921 Ley Line Theory.

Poltergeist Hauntings

The word poltergeist comes from the German words Poltern ("to make a racket") and Geist ("ghost"), and the term itself literally means "noisy ghost". In actuality a poltergeist is really not a ghost at all in the traditional sense. A poltergeist is actually thought to be a creation, caused by Psychokinesis, emanating most often from an adolescent girl living within the household. Seldom, if ever, does the person responsible for the activity even realize they are the source. While young males and adults have also exhibited the same phenomenon, it is not the norm. It's generally thought that the person responsible is going through a temporary emotional disturbance created by some sort of real or perceived trauma, or even possibly something as simple as a hormonal imbalance (adolescent development).

A poltergeist will normally manifest itself, at first, in simple mischievous ways, such as by knocking sounds or simple movement of objects. Manifestations can quickly escalate though to the movement of heavy objects, property destruction, physical attack, and starting of fires. It's generally believed too that the emotional energy created by fear within the other members of the household actually feeds and magnifies the activity even more. Full-blown poltergeist activity can be potentially very dangerous to be around, so tread with care.

One of the best ways to determine if the haunting is from a true poltergeist is to remove the person thought to be causing the activity from the premises. If the activity diminishes markedly or stops, you pretty much know you're dealing with a poltergeist. Since poltergeist activity is host dependent it can disappear as quickly as it began, and may also relocate to a new residence along with the creator host to start again. Usually poltergeist activity will cease on its own as the creator host gets older, but not always.

There are some within the paranormal community who believe that poltergeists can be created or perpetuated by what I would term "group think". In other words; if enough people actually believe something exists and project enough psychic energy towards that thought, then a manifestation will result. That may answer the question of why certain supposedly haunted houses and hotels have had the same type of poltergeist activity across multiple generations and multiple owners. To quote Napoleon Hill - "Whatever the mind can conceive and believe, it can achieve."

In 1996, Ike Clanton, decedent of the original Ike Clanton of OK Corral fame dressed in cowboy attire had his friend photograph him while he stood in Boot Hill Graveyard in Tombstone, Arizona. After reviewing the photograph, Clanton noticed a man in the background of the photo that was not there when the photograph was taken. Clanton was intrigued by this and set out to recreate the photo with a friend standing in the background and discovered it was impossible to recreate the picture without having the legs visible. This photograph remains a mystery to this day.

Treat it like a Crime Scene

From my perspective, because of my education and background in criminal justice, security management, and forensics; I tend to approach "ghost hunting" as a detective would in investigating a crime. You research and analyze the scene, interview potential witnesses, collect both hard (objective/documentary) and soft (circumstantial/subjective) evidence, and put it all together to try and make your case. Everything is done for a reason, usually in the same approximate order, to make sure every aspect of the investigation is thoroughly covered and reviewed. In other words, you should always approach any investigation in a systematic way and try to leave no stone unturned.

One of the best ways I know to keep everything on track and running smoothly is to develop and use a set of before, during, and after investigation checklists. Now whether you keep that information on your laptop or on a printed paper checklist (recommended) is up to you, but I assure you a checklist system will help immeasurably. It's not a happy time when you're 100 miles from home ready to set up and find out that "somebody" forgot to bring the cases with all the digital recorders and extra batteries. You laugh, but it's happened. Develop and use checklists religiously and you won't be faced with that situation.

The job of the detective, or in this case the paranormal investigator, is to attempt to answer the; who, what, where, when, and why of the haunting. Just like with many criminal investigations you start with limited information and then bit by bit you attempt to put a picture together that makes sense; which you can then take to the prosecuting attorney. Frequently though that picture remains incomplete no matter how hard you work at it. You may know in your heart of hearts what the truth is, but you just can't conclusively prove it to others. Just remember though, lots of people get convicted with only circumstantial evidence every day. Ghost hunting is similar in respect to circumstantial evidence. You may not necessarily have the "smoking gun", but you still may be able to collect enough "credible" circumstantial evidence to make a good case.

Investigating anomalous and generally non-duplicable activity is both exciting and frustrating at the same time. That's why it's so important to develop a systematic and workable game plan that will allow you the best opportunity to gather that hard credible evidence we all relish. Start with the What, When, and Where, learn everything you can about each, then move on to the Who and Why. If you don't like the crime scene analogy, just think of it like a giant 1000 piece jigsaw puzzle without the picture on the box of how it's supposed to look when finished. You simply start with the easy similarly colored sections and slowly work your way thru until the picture finally reveals itself.

The problem you'll find with ghost hunting is that virtually all your evidence is going to be circumstantial and subjective. You may KNOW that you been pushed, had your hair pulled, saw the shadow figure, heard a disembodied voice, or any number of other things – but the bottom line is that without hard evidence, such as a photograph, video, or readily discernible EVP it's only a circumstantial and subjective (personal) experience. It doesn't mean that it didn't happen; it just means that it's yours alone, which of itself is still pretty darn cool.

Here's something to always keep in mind. Don't be predisposed to fully believing in unsupported facts or fanciful tales told by others. Many times the commonly told story is at a minimum at least partially wrong. This is true especially in local haunts that are not well documented or investigated. Wrong names, wrong dates, and wrong locations happen more often than you think. Dig deep and the true facts will usually reveal themselves.

It can't be stressed enough that you need to take concise notes and log everything. Do not ever rely on memory alone!!!

This photo was taken by Tony O'Rahilly in Shropshire, England; after a devastating fire had gutted a number of buildings in the town. There was no one in this building at the time, yet this photo shows a young girl peering out. The photo was examined by Dr. Vernon Harrison, the former president of the Royal Photographic Society. Harrison deemed that the photo had not been tampered with and was therefore genuine. In 1677, a young girl named Jane Churn died in a fire she accidentally set, that burned down many of the town's old timber houses.

Pre-Investigative Research

Without a doubt, pre-investigative research is probably the most important segment in any professional paranormal investigation. It's what separates the men from the boys, so to speak. Granted, it can take hours and hours to do sometimes, but it is well worth it in the end. Unless you are willing to devote the time and effort into thoroughly researching the history of the property, events, and people attached before conducting an investigation, you may want to resign yourself to the fact that you're simply a thrill seeker and not a real investigator.

It simply amazes me sometimes how many haunting claims have so little basis in truth, even some of the more celebrated ones. Once told though, they tend to take on a life of their own, embellished with untrue or distorted facts meant to catch the imagination of the thrill seeking public, and must I say, the thrill seeking pseudo-investigator. Don't fall into the trap of accepting the supposed facts presented to you as gospel without taking the time to verify, if at all possible.

While it may seem trivial and nit picking, not to mention a whole bunch of extra work, to delve further into either an established well-known story or a current client's claims, it's not. Your goal is to attempt to ascertain the truth, plain and simple. That's why the best paranormal investigators always maintain a healthy dose of skepticism, take nothing at face value, and do their own research. Just having "faith" in the "purported" facts of the case is not enough. Remember, the definition of faith is, at least in this context is; belief - in the absence of real proof.

The great thing about researching is that, for the most part, your sources will be free to use. Your only charge being for any paper copies you make. The best freebie starting points are the library, the city/county newspaper, the local historical society, and the local city/county Recorder of Deeds. You'll be amazed at what you can dig up concerning the particular property you're investigating including; previous ownership records, current and past property usage, birth and deaths records, marriage records, genealogical records, relevant events that may have occurred on or near the property, historical photographs, maps, and on and on and on.

You also will want to talk to (interview), if at all possible, any past owners/residents, friends, family, or anyone else for that matter that may have relevant and pertinent information, that wouldn't be found in the public archives. Sometimes there may be an initial reluctance to discuss certain events or family history but usually with a little coaxing even the most reclusive and reluctant are willing to share what they know. Don't forget to follow up with the obligatory thank you note, or if you're lazy a thank you call, to let them know you appreciate them taking time to help. Not only is it common courtesy, but you never know if you may need to touch base again on a follow-up investigation or maybe a new investigation in the same area.

You may have noticed that I didn't include the Internet in my list of free go-to research sources. Contrary to popular belief, the Internet is not the "repository of all knowledge and information" it's made out to be, especially for the type of hard core, and truthful, historical information you're looking for here. Granted, it's a good place to start when you're looking for new locations to investigate, initial cursory background information, maps and direction, etc., but that's about it. Within this context the really useful, relevant, and truthful information you need, if it is even available on the Internet, is only going to be found on special databases or membership sites, both of which usually require you to pay for access privileges. Again not free, but it won't break the bank either.

A squadron of the Royal Air Force assembled to take a group photograph. After the picture was developed the squad quickly realized that this was no ordinary picture. Standing behind one of his mates was the recently deceased Freddy Jackson. Jackson was a mechanic for the Royal Air Force and served on-board the H.M.S. Daedalus. He had been working when we was killed in a freak-accident by an air plane propeller two days prior to the photo. Several of the other men in the photo confirmed that it was in fact Jackson's face in the background of the picture.

On-Site Evidence Gathering

At this point I'm going to assume, for this discussion, that you've located and procured a site to investigate, conducted a thorough background investigation on the claimed haunting including the property people and history, gathered your team and equipment, and have done a walk-through in daylight, or with the lights on, of the location to familiarize yourselves with where everything is including such things as; any potentially dangerous or out of bounds areas, location of power boxes and light switches, uneven or loose flooring, stairways, open broken or missing windows or doors, etc. that could factor in to your investigation. I'm also going to assume that you're investigating as a team, though pretty much all the information given in this book applies to the solo hunter too.

The initial walk-through is also a prime opportunity to gather your initial baseline EMF and temperature readings; determine stationary audio recorder and video camera locations, map known hotspots, and to figure out your overall investigative strategy. It's also a good idea at this time to take as many photographs of the property both inside and out for reference and comparison purposes. You never know what might show up in those pictures even before the investigation has even really started. I find reference photographs to be especially useful in determining, when questions arise, whether particular doors or windows were originally open or closed, and whether furniture or objects have been moved by possibly a team member, normally occurring physical activities such as gravity, uneven surfaces, or air movement, or whether it could possibly been some type of spirit activity.

I for one would also suggest that you or someone in your group make at least a quick sketch of the property/building noting the locations of each of the aforementioned items, at a minimum. If a blueprint, architectural drawing, map, or aerial photograph exists, then use them too. Over time many residential and commercial buildings have been remodeled and structurally altered. Sometimes, by simply using a tape measure and your observational skills, you'll find such things as doors or windows that have been relocated, hidden stairways or passageways, or even closed off rooms that no one living is aware of. Claims of the sounds of someone walking up or down stairs where none exists, or that of an apparition that apparently enters or exits at the same place through a now solid wall are now more believable when you realize that there actually was a staircase or doorway in that location, generations ago.

That also ties back to the fact of how important it is to know the past history of the property/building in question, what it has been used for over the years, along with what events, especially traumatic ones, that have occurred in, on, or adjacent to the property? As an example; the reported sights or sounds of music, people talking, clinking glasses, or apparitions of people in 1920s vintage clothing wouldn't make a lot of sense; that is unless you knew that the building, house, or location was actually that of a former speakeasy and gangster hangout during the 1920s.

The knowledge and information you acquire prior to the actual evidence gathering phase will allow you to better determine your strategy and focus. Do you stick with the known hotspots or try to cover the entire property? How should the available personnel and equipment be deployed? Should you focus on audio, photographic, or video evidence gathering; or simply use the shotgun approach? What type of haunting is most likely occurring? Those and a hundred additional questions can best be served by gathering all the information you can, prior to starting.

Now in a perfect world you would go into an investigation knowing everything there was to know about the location, every member of your team would be a no nonsense trained and experienced investigator, and you would have more than enough of the latest and greatest audio, video, photographic, and environmental detection equipment to cover every square inch of the property. Now we all know that that doesn't happen in the real world or for that matter even on many of the TV shows. In other words, you use what you have and utilize it to the maximum.

If you are a bare-bones operation with limited equipment you can offset that perceived disadvantage by knowing your equipment inside out and working smarter. I can tell you from experience that a dedicated, knowledgeable, and professionally oriented team with limited resources and equipment can run circles around the average highly funded team when it comes to actually gathering real quality evidence. Why? Because they know each other's strengths and weaknesses to a tee; they know what their equipment absolutely can and cannot do, and above all else they use their brains instead of simply and lazily relying on some high dollar piece of electronics. Don't fall into the trap of believing that the only way to be a good investigator is to have thousands and thousands of dollars in equipment lying around. If you do, you'll be wrong.

The size of the property being investigated, the number of team members you have, and the amount and type of equipment you have available will dictate whether the team operates individually or in pairs with whatever equipment they bring, or whether you set up a formal "command center" operation with a central monitoring station. Utilizing the command and control center system is the much preferred method if at all possible. Your command center can be as simple or as elaborate as you want depending on needs and equipment availability. The command center serves a myriad of purposes including: as being a centralized meeting/safety location, equipment storage area, real-time audio and video monitoring center, and team management/communication point.

Usually the command center is manned by one or possibly two people at any one time. The command center coordinator can either be dedicated (that's all they do for the entire investigation) or floating (everyone takes turns). Command center placement will vary from investigation to investigation depending on the physical size, location, and layout of the property. For all practical purposes you want it located in a spot away from audio and visual noise contamination, but still close enough to allow investigators easy access and communication. Generally the command center manager is in charge of all stationary equipment placement and operation, investigator placement, and communications coordination.

Before you start the actual investigation you'll need to have a team meeting to go over such things as; how the investigation is to be conducted, the roles of each investigator, rules of conduct, and to also do a thorough and complete equipment test to make sure everything is working properly and ready to go. At this time you should also make sure that all investigators are aware of any problem areas, hotspots, or any areas that may be deemed restricted or no access.

Whether it's your first or 100th investigation it never hurts to quickly go over your general team rules such as:

* No investigating alone.

* You must stay in visual contact with at least one other investigator at all times.

* No negative provocation at any time.

* Tag all audio recordings with investigator, time, and place at both the start and finish of each session.

* Talk at normal voice level – whispering can screw up an EVP session.

* Be respectful of the spirits, your fellow investigators, the property you are investigating, and the owner or client's wishes.

* Be aware of your surroundings at all times.

* If you get startled or scared Do Not Run ever – that's how most people get hurt.

* If you see something, hear something, feel something, or smell something out of the ordinary do not keep it to yourself.

While the aforementioned team rules are good place to start, you'll actually need to develop your own rules of conduct specific to your team and how you actually want to conduct your investigations. Remember, there are no set rules to abide by, unless you set them. Regardless of how you conduct your investigations you want to make sure that everybody is on the same page, and is operating in a cooperative and cohesive manner. With some groups it's a constant struggle to keep everybody on task all the time.

To be honest, neither I nor anyone else can give you an exact universal blueprint on how you should conduct your on-site investigations. There are just too many variables such as: investigative goals, team member makeup, experience, type of equipment you're using, etc. for any kind of standard "works every time" checklist to be used. The only things I can offer are suggestions and examples to point you in the right direction so you can, in the end, develop your own modus operandi (method of operation). Here is an example scenario to get you started on thinking about what an investigation entails:

Example Investigation Scenario:

You are ready to investigate an old (mid-1850s) occupied two-story home with basement and attic located in sparsely populated rural area. The owners/occupants have lived in the house for a few years and noticed activity from the moment they moved in. Activity has been reported both inside and outside the home by the owners, with the main hotspots being the first floor living room area, the stairway to the second floor, and one of the bedrooms on the second floor. Reported activity includes; disembodied voices, shadow figures, and full body apparitions of what appears to be men in some type of uniform. The owners are not afraid of the spirit activity and are only looking for some possible answers and validation. They have actually collected some pretty compelling EVP's and photographs themselves over the past couple of years, but you are the first actual professional ghost hunting group ever asked to investigate.

Your pre-investigative research has determined that: the current owners have no history of previous hauntings in their other residences, the past owner though reluctant to talk did confirm previous activity, there were no known murders or suicides found to have occurred on the property, a number of previous owners and family members died from natural causes on the property over the past 160 years and are buried in a cemetery located within a mile of the property, the house itself is primarily built on solid limestone bedrock, and the property is bordered on one side by a small river. Your historical research has concluded that this entire property was used several times as a Confederate encampment during the Civil War and that the house and surrounding grounds was most likely used as a hospital and/or field headquarters. Numerous Civil War soldiers are also buried in the cemetery that is nearby.

For this investigation your team consists of five members; three of which have tons of experience and two that are rather new. You have a full complement of detection equipment including: stationary IR video cameras with DVR, handheld video and still cameras, digital recorders, ambient temperature thermometers, EMF detectors, etc. You also have your laptop loaded with audio and video software to instantly review any captured audio or video evidence immediately. All additional needed equipment and other items such as flashlights, extra batteries, and the like are accounted for.

At this time you've completed your walk-through, gotten baseline EMF and temperature readings, and positioned your stationary IR video cameras to cover the known hotspots and the outside perimeter of the house. It was decided to set up a command center monitoring station in the kitchen that will be manned by one team member continuously throughout the entire investigation. A complete equipment check has been done with each member being assigned a digital audio recorder, a digital still camera, EMF detector, and an ambient temperature thermometer. Each team will also carry a digital IR/multi spectrum video recorder. Investigators will hunt in pairs with team one starting on the inside of the house, and team two starting outside. All team members have walkie-talkies for instant communication with each other. Teams will switch locations periodically so as to have each team investigate each floor of the house and the outside grounds individually. From this point on each of the teams will follow whatever prescribed investigative format you've chosen to follow.

It's now up to you to determine the best course of action, or format, your team will use to try and gather the best evidence possible...... In other words, do they start in the basement, first floor, second floor, or attic? Where and how far does your outside team wander? Do you want to concentrate on EVP's, photographic and video, or both? These are all things that you have to decide, prior to starting, based on a number of factors which could include: team member abilities, past experiences and successes, how much time that you have to spend at the location, etc., etc. With time and experience you'll instinctively know what the best avenue of attack will be. For now, I'm more interested in getting you to stop and think, instead of just reacting.

Keep in mind, every investigation that you do will be different. Even though you'll be basically following the same protocols and procedures, or operational framework as it were, each investigation will have its own unique characteristics, problems, and challenges. It's the fluid nature of paranormal investigations that makes it so challenging and exciting, yet maddening at the same time. Just when you think you have it figured out, you realize you don't and must change your game plan to fit the current requirements. No luck with EVP's on the digital recorder? Maybe it's time to bring out the spirit box or Ovilus if you have one. Separate teams not working? Maybe it's time to bring everybody together to investigate as one big group. Never be afraid to mix it up and try different things if you see the need.

Training Exercise

At this time I want you to do a little creative thinking and try to put yourself more into the investigative mindset by doing several exercises in the exact listed order I'm giving you.

FIRST - Go back to the beginning of the example scenario and reread it again slowly, sentence by sentence. As you do this, make believe that you are the case manager/team leader going over actual true case facts and laying out how your investigation is to proceed. Think as you are reading; Does it make sense? Do I need to add anything? Get yourself a pen and paper and make notes if you need to. List questions and comments about the scenario itself; what's right and what's wrong about it. Literally picture in your mind the whole scenario as if it were true. Visualize yourself actually at the location, imagine the research you've done, see the equipment in front of you, and actually picture yourself going over the scenario with your team members at command central. Once you reach the point where you can actually put yourself on location and inside the narrative, you'll start to make instant connections and assumptions as to how to logically proceed.

SECOND - The next thing I need you to do is to watch a little TV. Now that may sound strange coming from a book author, but believe me it's not and will make a whole lot of sense once you do it. I want you to pick three or four different ghost hunting shows such as; Ghost Hunters, Ghost Adventures, Dead Files, Haunted Collector, etc. that you like. Now randomly pick a couple episodes of each to watch. It doesn't matter if you've seen them before. Granted these shows are great entertainment, but for this exercise entertainment is not the number one priority. What I want you to do is to analyze each of the shows in respect to their investigative techniques, use of equipment, investigative protocols, and general demeanor as they conduct their investigations. Look at what they do with a very critical eye. Again, get out your pen and paper and make notes if you need to. Ask yourself; are they using that equipment in the correct manner, could they make better use of their time and efforts, what's their actual game plan, does it make sense to do that, and more than anything – how would I, as an investigator, do that differently and better.

THIRD - Your final exercise will be a real eye-opener. I want you to get on the Internet and do some digging. What you're looking for will be videos of real investigations posted on any of the ghost hunting group's websites or on YouTube that actually show teams in the field interacting with each other, using various pieces of equipment, reviewing evidence, etc. They need to be long enough so you can actually get a good view of how the team works. Quick little clips just showing purported evidence don't count. Your job will be to analyze these videos in the same way you did with the television shows, with a very critical eye. I then want you to divide the videos you watch into three categories: (1) These guys look like they're doing everything correctly and I want to emulate them. (2) These guys look like they kind of know what they're doing but need some fine tuning. (3) OMG - These guys are a disaster and need some real help. Again, put your thinking cap on and ask; "how would I, as an investigator, do that differently and better?"

Once you've done these three exercises you'll have a leg up on just about every new investigator, and a large number of so-called experienced investigators. Why, because you've actually taken the time to question and analyze, rather than simply regurgitate back facts that may or may not be correct in the first place. The goal here is not for me to tell you "my" right way to do something and you blindly follow it. You have to understand, in paranormal investigations especially, that "you" have to ultimately decide "your own" right way of doing things. Liken it to having 10 great singers sing the same song. Technically it's the same song, but you'll get 10 distinctly different interpretations.

Once you have gotten to the point where you recognize and understand the basics, can discern between good and poor application in the field, and are able to think and adapt; you'll be able to develop "your own" methods and procedures that will fit you and your team's wants, needs, and abilities. I referred to that before, you'll recall, as "Mastering the Basics".

Debunking

Part of your job as an investigator is to determine if there is a rational natural alternative explanation for an event that has occurred such as; a door opening or closing, a window closing, perceived knocks or footsteps, object rolling across the floor, drastic temperature changes, electromagnetic spikes, light or sound anomalies, etc. That does not mean that you have to spend an inordinate amount of time or effort running around trying to track every tiny perceived anomaly like some deranged cat after an elusive mouse. That's counterproductive to your investigation. Conversely, you can't take the attitude that absolutely everything that you see or hear during an investigation is always paranormal in nature.

Here are a few examples of supposed paranormal activity that may in fact have a more logical and non-ghostly source.....

(1) Claimed/Experienced: Banging, knocking, or rapping sounds
Possible Cause: Air in water pipes, loose doors or windows, tree branches, heating/ac fan or ducting

(2) Claimed/Experienced: Toilet flushing or faucet tuning on by it self

Possible Cause: Faulty valve or seal, water pressure too high or fluctuating

(3) Claimed/Experienced: Doors opening or closing on their own

Possible Cause: Faulty door alignment, building tilt, vacuum created by opening or closing an exterior door, vibration, floor flex

(4) Claimed/Experienced: Windows opening or closing on their own

Possible Cause: Gravity, faulty latch, or faulty alignment

(5) Claimed/Experienced: Lights flickering or turning off and on by themselves

Possible Cause: Faulty wiring, loose bulb, faulty switch, corroded connection

(6) Claimed/Experienced: Objects falling off shelves or counter tops

Possible Cause: Surface not level, vibration, air movement, slick surface

(7) Claimed/Experienced: Smells and Odors

Possible Cause: Sources are too varied to list. Be aware that odors and smells can carry quite a distance depending on wind, temp, and humidity

(8) Claimed/Experienced: Electronics or appliances turning off or on by themselves

Possible Cause: Faulty wiring, faulty switch, bad timer, loose connection

(9) Claimed/Experienced: Sounds of walking, scratching, or creaking

Possible Cause: Tree branches, building settling, animals

(10) Claimed/Experienced: Hearing voices or conversations

Possible Cause: Voices and sounds can carry quite far, especially at night, and can be magnified and funneled by such things as hard surfaces, room/building design, ductwork, and location

(11) Claimed/Experienced: Shadows and light anomalies

Possible Cause: Possible light from exterior sources such as passing automobiles, street lights, or lighted signs. Windows, mirrors, and smooth surfaces may reflect light and create moving shadows

(12) Claimed/Experienced: Various and sundry physical and mental health issues which may be present including: cancer, skin and respiratory problems, headaches, nausea, fatigue, hallucinations, depression, dizziness, and paranoia
Possible Cause: Check for the presence of extremely high EMF levels, carbon monoxide, mold, toxic cleaning chemicals, asbestos, pesticides, and rodent/insect infestations

To quote Sherlock Holmes; "'It is a capital mistake to theorize before one has data. Insensibly one begins to twist facts to suit theories, instead of theories to suit facts". In other words, make sure your conclusions are based, to the highest degree possible, on facts; not simply unsubstantiated conjecture or feelings.

Group or Solo Investigations?

As to why and how you conduct your ghost hunting, that's up to you, plain and simple. Some will argue that the only way to properly ghost hunt is to join an established group, use all the latest high-tech equipment, and properly document every action. Practically speaking, that's usually the best way to go. In a group setting; you have the safety in numbers factor, you can draw on other members experience and expertise, different tasks can be spread around, and more than anything – you get to hang around with like-minded people and have a good time.

As far as going it alone in being your own solitary one-person team, that's okay too, within limits. Solo hunters face a much greater risk of injury and potentially life-threatening problems occurring than groups do. This is especially true on night hunts or when investigating abandoned buildings or areas in sparsely populated locations. The solo hunter has no immediate backup help to come to their rescue and would have to rely on their cell phone to call for assistance. If you're going to solo hunt then I would suggest using extreme caution and common sense. Don't be a statistic. It's not worth it.

Quite frankly, a great part of my research and investigative time over the years has been spent as a solo "lone-wolf" team, for better or worse. Granted, I have gotten myself into numerous sticky situations, and I can't necessarily recommend that you do it, but so far I have survived. Even when I've been fortunate enough to team hunt, I've always tried to keep the numbers low, usually three to five total to keep it manageable. That way you can have one person acting as coordinator and equipment/safety monitor while allowing one or two pairs to actually investigate at any one time.

Day or Night Time Investigations?

The same also goes for nighttime versus day time hunting, it's up to you. While there may be solid scientific or practical reasons for choosing to hunt at night, daytime hunts can also be as productive, depending on location.

Hunting at night has become the de facto standard for a number of reasons; it's generally quieter, there's less pedestrian and vehicle traffic, it's somewhat easier to control the environment, it's much more creepy and scary, and many times, especially if it's an occupied dwelling or business, it may simply be the only time it's available. It also may be a case where that's the only time your group can get together. There are two reasons why I believe night hunting is the preferred time by most; the inherent creepiness factor and the belief that the veil of communication between the spiritual and physical planes is weakest during the dead of night. Whether the latter is true or not is questionable.

All things being equal, and given the choice, I would prefer starting with a thorough and complete daytime investigation and then move to a nighttime hunt if I felt it was warranted. Quite frankly I don't believe that ghosts take the day off and only come out at night. Stumbling around in a pitch black building or cemetery with a small flashlight or a limited range IR camera, or rushing back and forth to every perceived sound or light anomaly may make for great edge of the seat TV viewing but in all honesty the slow, thoughtful, and methodical investigator operating in a non-blacked out environment will gather more quality evidence in the long run, and do it much more safely. Just my opinion, so take it for what it's worth.

Dealing with Property Owners and Clients

The number one and two rules to always remember are "Always Ask Permission and Never Trespass". In fact, tattoo that on your forehead so you'll never forget. Nothing will ruin your day or weekend quicker than getting arrested or having a gun pointed at you because you stupidly decided to investigate some abandoned house or other building without checking with the owner first. In fact, in pretty much all states, if a building is involved, you can actually be charged with a host of seriously nasty things, like felony burglary. Try explaining that to your cell mates at the county jail. Be aware too that different states have varying trespass signage posting requirements ranging from basically none to very specific.

From my experience, if you approach a property owner in a professional and respectful manner, you will get a yes about a third of the time, maybe. Not as much as you'd like, but then again consider a professional baseball player would kill to average one hit out of three at-bats, so it's all relative. There are a thousand reasons why an owner doesn't want you wandering around on his or her property. What the owner's reason is doesn't matter, and quite frankly, is none of your business. So if you get a no, just thank them for their time, and go on down the road.

Even if you're investigating in the open on public property, you'll need to make sure that you know all the do's and don'ts rules and regulations that are specific to the location, any city ordinances, or state laws. If you're on federal property, they go by another set of rules entirely. Now if you think I'm preaching to you on this subject, you are correct.

Since this book is written for beginning or novice investigators I'm only going to touch on the subject of clients and client relationships very briefly. I would hope that until you have the knowledge and get some real hands-on experience that you would refrain from taking on any client requested investigations that would be residential in nature and involve families.

You have to understand that when somebody contacts you to investigate their home, or even business, it's usually not just for fun and games. Clients are concerned or even scared of what's happening around them and are looking for help, guidance, and answers. That takes not only investigative experience, but some very good counseling skills too.

Now if you've been asked by a client to investigate an abandoned or unoccupied property or building, with no direct human involvement or interaction taking place, then that can be a different situation entirely. Instead of you having to look for an abandoned or unoccupied property or building to investigate and then having to ask permission to do so, the owner has actually come to you. Count yourself very fortunate.

While it doesn't completely relieve you of any responsibility to act in a professional manner and report your findings back to the client, you will be able to operate in a slightly looser manner than you would in say a residential/family setting. Look at it like just another good learning/skills building experience.

Once you reach the point of feeling comfortable in your abilities to take on client requested investigations, you'll need to reevaluate your entire organization and upgrade, if you will, to a more professional and businesslike approach, if you haven't done so already. What that means is you need to take a look at everything from A-Z; how initial research is conducted, personnel suitability; equipment needs, investigative protocols, evidence evaluation procedures, etc., etc. Once you cross that threshold you owe it to the client, yourself, and the paranormal community as a whole to always conduct yourself in an appropriate and professional manner; that is if you ever want to be taken seriously.

Equipment

One of the biggest fallacies in ghost hunting is that you need to have all kinds of high-tech equipment to be successful. While having access to all the latest and greatest gizmos and gadgets available will certainly facilitate and enhance your investigations, if used properly and for their intended purpose, you have to realize that the single most important piece of equipment you can possess is your brain. Your five senses and observational skills can never be replaced by a simple device; enhanced yes, replaced never.

It's also important that you absolutely understand the fact that there is no single piece of equipment of any kind that will detect the presence of a spirit, per se. Repeat - there is no single piece of equipment in existence that definitively detects ghosts. Anyone who tells you otherwise is full of crap. The detection equipment we use in ghost hunting (i.e. EMF detectors, digital thermometers, motion detectors, etc) detect and measure changes (anomalies) in the environment, nothing more. The changes (anomalies) that are then collectively found during an investigation, especially those that we can't find any rational alternative scientific explanation for; may then in fact be used to deductively determine or at least infer, the possible presence of a spirit or spirits.

It bears repeating; *"while we may not be able to scientifically prove their existence at any given place or time using currently existing detection equipment, we can infer their existence thru the changes that do occur - that can't otherwise be explained rationally or scientifically"*. Couple that with a compelling EVP or photographic/video capture and you hit the jackpot.

The type and amount of ghost hunting equipment you will have is dependent on how much you're willing to spend, plain and simple. Don't fall into the trap though of thinking that simply by virtue of owning that new shiny gizmo you'll somehow be a better investigator. You won't. Unless you actually put in the practice and become totally familiar with the capabilities and limitations of a particular piece of equipment, it can actually hinder your investigations. Another problem with depending strictly on high end electronic gizmos and gadgets is their tendency to fail at the most inopportune time. If you're like too many investigators, it's all over; simply because you never really took the time or made the effort to learn and remember the low-tech basics.

Liken it to two carpenters; one with only a hammer and a hand saw, the other with a nail gun and a power saw. Both are knowledgeable and competent carpenters, but what happens if the power goes out? The first carpenter goes on, while the second carpenter, who is totally dependent on his "high-tech" power equipment, is dead in the water and out of work.....Kind of a cheesy analogy I know, but the morals here are pretty clear: #1 - Don't rely entirely on gadgets and gizmos to do the work for you, it makes you lazy. #2 - Be prepared for the worst case scenario and don't be afraid to go "low-tech" if you have to. #3 - Always use your brain; it's the one piece of equipment that won't fail you.

Here's a fairly good list of investigative equipment and support items that I've found to be useful over the years and that will get you started. I've divided the items into two main sections: Basic Necessities - Support Items and Monitoring - Documentation Equipment. Remember, this isn't an all-inclusive list, nor is it a required list. Your particular needs and requirements may be much smaller or larger, depending on the size and scope of your investigations and to a large degree your budgetary constraints. My suggestion is to start small, become very proficient with the basics, and then slowly start building your investigative equipment arsenal up by adding to and becoming totally proficient with, one piece at a time.

BASIC NECESSITIES AND SUPPORT ITEMS
First Aid Kit

Gloves

Wristwatch

Maps

Flashlights

Bug Repellent

Batteries

Tape Measure

Notebook and Pen

Level

Beverages/Snacks

Masking Tape

Safety Glasses

Glow Sticks

Equipment Vest

Chalk

Sturdy Clothing/Footwear

Twist Ties

Lens Cleaner

Talcum Powder

ID

Cotton Balls

Cell Phone

Twine

Walkie-Talkies

Ziploc Bags

Multi Tool

Small Tool Kit

Dust Mask

Lock Lid Plastic Storage Boxes

Compass

Candles

Most everything listed as necessities and support items is pretty much self-explanatory if you think about it. What you may not realize is that among that list are all the items you need to conduct a "low-tech" investigation. A compass can be used as a poor man's EMF detector, cotton balls or candles for air movement, talcum powder as a motion detector, chalk to mark object position, etc. Ask yourself this, "What did the paranormal investigators of old use before the advent of electronic detection equipment?" Answer – It wasn't anything that was battery powered!

Now I'm not advocating going the low-tech route if you don't have to, but it's nice to know that you have the ability to adapt to and compensate for situations where your standard electronic equipment fails or where you don't have enough high-tech equipment to fully cover the location. This all comes back around again to "mastering the basics" and being able to adapt and think on your feet, instead of just throwing in the towel because boohoo, your battery died.

MONITORING & DOCUMENTATION EQUIPMENT

K-II EMF Meter - Fast sampling Electromagnetic field (EMF) meter that covers frequencies from 30-20,000 Hz. Great instrument for both Paranormal Research and for finding potentially harmful high EMF levels in your home or work environment.

Tri-Field Natural EM Meter - The TriField Natural EM Meter was designed to do field measurements for special research. It detects changes in extremely weak static (DC or "natural") electric and magnetic fields, and signals with both a tone and the movement of a needle-type gauge if either the electric or magnetic field changes from previous levels.

Mel Meter - Intelligent microprocessor based instrument specifically designed for Paranormal Investigators & Enthusiasts. The Mel Meter incorporates various different features that are combined into a durable unit designed to be operated with only one hand. Able to record EMF and Temperature simultaneously.

IR/Ambient Temperature Gun - IRT642 Hybrid/ Precision IR & Ambient Temperature Gun Combination Instrument with Laser sight. IR Thermometer measures both non-contact surfaces using a laser target and measures ambient temperature simultaneously.

Motion Detector - There are basically three types of sensors used: Passive Infrared Sensor (PIR), Ultrasonic (active) Sensor, and Microwave (active) Sensor. The most common motion detector for ghost hunting is usually the 'Passive infrared sensor' type but some ghost hunters use ultrasonic and microwave sensors as well or in combination. The reason why passive infrared sensors or PIR are used the most is because they detect body heat and no energy is emitted from the sensor.

Laser Grid Light

Laser Grid Pen - High powered laser emits a grid of green dots useful for detecting shadows or general visual disturbances during an investigation. Set it in front of a running camera to catch potential evidence. You can adjust the size and shape of the stars by turning the adjustable lens. Detach the lens and it will function as a high powered laser pointer.

Full Spectrum Digital Camera - Full-spectrum cameras can detect visible, near-infrared, and near-ultraviolet light. Advantages to using Full Spectrum cameras are that when you use them you do not need to use a flash which eliminates capturing false anomalies, such as, orbs e.g., dust, moisture, pollen, and reflections. A major disadvantage to using a Full Spectrum camera versus a normal camera is they cast a pink glow in daylight or natural lighting.

Full Spectrum Digital Camcorder - Professionally modified 1080p HD Camcorder that can be used as a regular camcorder, "IR MODE" similar to Sony NightShot models or "FULL SPECTRUM MODE" that enables sensitivity to Ultraviolet, Visible, and Infrared light. Three separate modes of operation: Regular Camcorder, IR Mode, and Full Spectrum Mode. An external infrared or full spectrum light is always recommended.

Digital Audio Recorder - Besides the Mel Meter, my most used piece of equipment. Make sure you get the best voice recorder you can afford. You'll also want good quality headphones to listen to your recordings. The Olympus recorder pictured has

Live EVP Listening Capability (when using headphones or external speaker).

These are my workhorse tools that I use most often. Your actual list of equipment can be much longer or shorter depending on your wants, needs, and budget. This is actually a small list of the actual equipment that I have, but what I've found over the years is that most people usually gravitate to a small handful of most used tools, while everything else sits on a shelf gathering dust and only gets pulled out on the rare occasion. If I had to shorten my list further, as to most needed and most used, I'd have to pick my digital recorder and Mel meter. Throw in a regular digital camera and some audio software for EVP's, and you'll be good to go. As your needs dictate and your budget allows, you can then start adding and upgrading your equipment.

One thing I need to mention, that nobody really pays attention to, is the amount of time needed to adequately review your photographic, video, and audio recordings. Let's say you have five people investigating for 10 hours; each of them collecting three or five hours of audio recording, taking 50 to 100 photographs, and recording an hour or two of video. Couple that with six stationary video cameras constantly recording for 10 hours. Given that scenario alone you'll have probably somewhere between 80 and 100 hours of total review time to take into account for a single investigation.

Just remember this simple fact when thinking of adding that big stationary multi-camera setup, stationary audio recorders in every room, and the like; for every hour of recording, plan on spending approximately the same time reviewing. Granted there are numerous ways to drastically cut down the review process such as; doing live playback EVP sessions only, doing live video monitoring/review during the investigation, using motion activated cameras, etc., but as a general rule of thumb the one hour to one hour figure will hold true for most investigations.

Again, I can't stress enough, with whatever equipment you use, that you take the time to thoroughly know both its capabilities and limitations before starting. Simply reading the manufacturer's directions booklet won't cut it. You will also have to devote a lot of hours of practice time to become really proficient.

EVP's (Electronic Voice Phenomena)

For thousands of year's communication with the dead was limited to the shamans, oracles, high priests, witches, medicine men, psychics, and mediums who would listen to, interpret, and pass on the information received from the other side, usually to the wealthy and powerful ruling classes who demanded it. That information then influenced decisions made by rulers ranging from when and where to grow certain crops to when and how wars and battles were to be fought. If we think about it, human history has been influenced and altered by decisions determined, at least in small part, from communication with the spirit world; be it actually real or imagined. For the most part historically, the average person was either oblivious to the possibility, taught to fear it religiously, or threatened by the state, much of the time under penalty of torture and death, from any form of participation.

As time went on, knowledge increased, civilization evolved, and the harsh restrictions were eased and rescinded. The average person was finally afforded third-party access to the spirit world thru the various available psychics, mediums, fortune tellers, tarot readers, and the like – all for a small monetary compensation, but still far short of any direct one on one audio communication we may be able to experience now. Today, technology has advanced to the point where actual voices from the spirit world can now be captured on a simple, widely available, and relatively inexpensive hand held digital recorder by virtually anyone who cares to try. The entire process by which ghostly voices and noises are captured and analyzed carries the cutesy, but aptly named, moniker of Electronic Voice Phenomena or EVP.

Generally speaking, Electronic Voice Phenomena (EVP) is the recording of human sounding voices on tape or digital recorders from an unknown source that are not generally heard by the person recording it. Only upon playback are these voices heard, usually in frequency ranges above or below normal human hearing. That's the simple definition. The more expansive definition would include any vocalized sounds such as; words, phrases, sentences, screams, grunts, groans, growling, or whistling; heard or unheard at the time of recording, that is of unknown origin, from any type of electronic recording device.

Instrumental communication with the dead is thought to have caught hold back in the 1920s when Thomas Edison postulated about the possibility of building a machine that could capture disembodied voices beyond this earthly plane. Whether he ever succeeded, or even attempted to build such a machine, is unknown. Actual experiments to try and capture spirit voices by others were not successful until the late 1930s. Over the decades since, the progression of technology from phonograph record cutters, vacuum tube radios, wire recorders, tape recorders, and on to digital recorders; communication, and to some degree interactive communication, with the spirit world is now readily available to every ghost hunter everywhere.

The quality of EVP's that you may record will vary from easily heard and understood to indistinguishable gibberish. They may sound mechanical or natural, may be in a foreign language, and can vary in gender, age, tone, emotion, and even accent. Many times audio amplification and noise filtering will have to be utilized and even then it may not be readily discernible.

Most researchers categorize EVP's according to this scale:

Class A - This type of EVP is loud, clear, and of very high quality. The voice is easily understandable and does not need enhancement or amplification. You'll find that Class A EVPs are often in direct response to a question being asked.

Class B - This is the most common type of EVP you'll find. They are lower in quality and clarity than a Class A, but are still generally very audible to the average person, especially when using headphones. Enhancement may or not be required. You'll find that Class B EVPs are more often not in direct response to a question.

Class C - This is the lowest quality EVP (garbage). Even the best enhancement is usually not sufficient enough for any type of real clarity. Generally, a Class C EVP, in my opinion, should never even be remotely considered as any type of evidence of the paranormal.

I have seen lists that show a dozen or more different types and categories of EVP's, which to me is a little ridiculous. As far as I'm concerned, if it's not Class A or Class B it's not worth my time and effort to go further. You can literally spend hours trying to pull up every little errant and indistinguishable blip or noise hoping against hope that you'll find something, but I'll guarantee you that 99.9999% of the time it's simply garbage.

Let me repeat; unless an EVP is readily discernible or discernible with just a little enhancement, disregard it. To do otherwise is an exercise in futility. You also have to realize your credibility as a Ghost Hunter and Paranormal Investigator is on the line every time you present purported evidence to clients, other researchers, or the public at large to judge; so go for only the best and most compelling.

Recording EVP's

First of all you'll need to obtain the best quality digital recorder that you can afford and make sure the recording quality setting is at its highest. I personally prefer a recorder with live playback capability so you can listen in real time and not have to wait till later after you download your audio files to your computer. You'll also need, especially if you're using a live playback recorder, a good set of headphones or external speaker. Also, depending on the particular recorder that you're using, you may want to think about getting a high quality, and much more sensitive, external omnidirectional microphone to use with it.

Basically there are two ways the recorder is used; as a mobile device and as a stationary device. Most people prefer to actually hold the recorder in their hand while recording. It allows you more freedom of movement as you go from spot to spot around the property or building you're investigating. The major drawback is that extraneous noise can be introduced into the recording by the physical handling of the recorder and your physical movements from place to place, if you're not careful. That's why it's important that you practice holding your recorder properly while recording and that you learn to tag, or identify, what is happening when you or others move about.

Your recorder can also be simply placed on a table, shelf, the floor, or even mounted on a tripod to be used as a stationary device. This is helpful if you're planning on staying in a particular area for an extended period or if you want to set up remote unattended recorders around the building and property. I've personally found it advantageous, if you're going to use stationary recorders, to take the time before you start your investigation to turn your recorders on and walk through the building room to room, tagging each, while carrying on a normal conversation. Then go back and replay each recorder so you'll have an idea of what the recorder is picking up and how normal distant sounds and movement are being recorded. You'll be surprised at how sounds can carry long distances and make you think many times that something paranormal is going on, while in truth, they're actually emanating from you or one of your team in another room or on another floor.

100

One of the biggest problems most people have when recording EVP's is learning to keep as quiet as possible. Extraneous noise sources from excessive talking; walking about, electronic devices, and other equipment can override and cancel out your recordings if you're not careful. What generally happens in an investigation is that everybody's all hyped up because it's dark and kind of creepy, no one can stay seated or standing in one place for over 10 seconds, and everybody wants to continually comment or whisper among themselves. In allowing this to happen, your opportunity to record discernible EVP's is greatly diminished and will add hours of additional and unneeded review time.

Once you're ready to go, hit the record button and begin by stating out loud; your name, the name of any other team member with you, where you are at, and what time it is. You'll want to do this for every recording session during an investigation. When you change rooms or location you'll need to make sure to verbally tag that location. If you choose to keep your recorder on while you are moving from place to place, be sure to verbally tag that too, so when you review your recordings later you'll be able to quickly differentiate between sounds emanating from your movements and those that are potentially paranormal in nature. You'll also want to tag any noises and sounds that you hear during a recording session such as: conversations from another room or another part of the building, horns honking or road traffic sounds, air conditioning or heating units going on and off, etc.

As far as questioning goes, I like to keep it conversational, friendly, and to the point. The first thing I do is introduce myself and anyone with me, state basically why we're here, and that we have no ill intentions and are only looking for answers. I like to keep questions very simple and pointed, and that can be answered in as few words as possible. Examples would be; "Are there any spirits here that would like to talk?", "Can you tell me your name?", "Did you used to live/work here?", "What year did you die?", "Did you die from natural causes or were you killed?" etc. If you have information or knowledge as to the particular spirit or spirits that may be haunting location, then you can personalize your questions more. "Is Mary here?", "Are you the lady in the white dress that's been seen at the top of the stairs?", or "Are you a member of the Jones family?"

After each question you'll want to wait maybe 5 to 10 seconds before asking another. This gives the spirit enough time to answer. If there's more than one of you conducting the EVP session you should always alternate the asking of questions between all the people present. Occasionally you'll find that there will be one person in your group that the spirits respond to better at that particular investigation site.

If you're using a regular digital recorder that does not have live playback you may want to occasionally stop your questioning, rewind, and replay to see if you have anything that really stands out, like a direct response to one of your questions. If I'm using a regular digital recorder I like to do this sometimes after maybe 8 to 10 questions. Sometimes you'll get responses, and sometimes not. When it comes to the paranormal, the only thing that you can really expect ever, is the unexpected.

One thing I would caution you against doing; and that is using negative provocation. In most cases challenging and provoking a spirit or spirits is not necessary and can sometimes have very negative consequences. It's not that I have never used provocation; I'm just saying that it should be used on a very selective basis. Unless otherwise indicated, you should always treat the spirits as you would any living breathing group of people, and that is with respect. Normally if you're nice, nonthreatening, and respectful you may be able capture some quality EVP's or even elicit direct answers to some of your questions. On the other hand if you are nasty and negative, you'll either be met by silence, threats, or worst-case scenario physical attack; same thing that you would expect to occur, if you were to walk into a crowded room of people anywhere and act like that. Just remember, it's hard to go wrong when you follow the Golden Rule.

Once you're finished it's now time to download your audio files to your computer for review. There are a number of free and paid audio software programs available that are relatively easy to use. Do a web search and try out several to find the one that best fits your needs and abilities. Any of these will allow you to be able to quickly scan, analyze, enhance, and amplify your audio files. Just remember what I mentioned earlier though about spending hours and hours of time trying to sort through pure garbage in hopes of finding some needle in the haystack, which may or may not in fact exist. Another thing to keep in mind is to be sure and save all your original audio files from each investigation for future reference. If, or I really should say when, you do find some real quality Class A or B EVP's be sure to share them with your fellow investigators and paranormal enthusiasts.

Photography and Video

If somebody were to ask me, "Have you ever taken a photograph or video of an actual ghost?" I'd have to answer no, in the strictest sense. Now if I were asked, "Have you ever taken photographs or video of visual anomalies such as; mists, orbs, light streaks, object movement, and shadows that I could not explain or immediately debunk as not being paranormal in origin?", then my answer would be yes. Were many of those photographs and videos of actual ghostly manifestations? While I can't definitively conclude, beyond a reasonable doubt "scientifically", that any of the photographs or videos that I've taken over the past several decades proves that; I would have to say, based on the totality of events surrounding and associated with these captures, that I'm convinced personally that many of the photographs and videos taken are of actual ghostly manifestations. How's that for equivocation?

Not to burst anyone's bubble but your chances of photographing or videotaping an actual clearly defined ghost that would meet "scientific" scrutiny is somewhere to the left of zero. Now would that same photograph or video meet the looser pseudoscientific standards of the paranormal community? Yes it would. Why? Because the paranormal community fully recognizes that we are dealing with random and non-duplicable anomalies and events. It all goes back to the endless science – pseudoscience debate that only makes sense to the narrow minded skeptics and disbelievers, who wouldn't acknowledge the existence of ghosts even if one came up and bit them on the ass. The quote that always pops into my mind is "Absence of evidence is not evidence of absence!"-Think about it. Whatever photographs or video captures you make will be for you, your team, and the paranormal community as a whole; not for the skeptics and disbelievers that have their minds closed shut to even the possibility.

Truthfully, concerning photography of any kind, I don't profess to be an expert; only a marginally proficient amateur. While everyone may have their own particular favorite type of camera, the fact is that virtually any camera you have at hand can be used to capture images of ghostly activity. You don't really need to invest in real expensive equipment to get started. Your little digital point and shoot camera will work just fine until you get some experience under your belt and then want to spend a little more money to upgrade. While high resolution digital IR or full spectrum capable cameras with powerful external lighting may be preferred, they are definitely not a requirement. If you are going to purchase a camera for ghost hunting it would behoove you to get one that has a very high megapixel rate and that is IR capable if possible. That way you'll be getting high-quality pictures and be able to shoot in virtually all light conditions. The most important thing though to know and remember is, with whatever still or video camera you use, become proficient with the equipment (yes, you'll have to actually read the directions and practice) and know its capabilities and limitations.

When it comes to ghost photography there is absolutely no best way, or absolute right way, of doing things. Some will tell you that it's best to use IR, in complete darkness; others will tell you that using flash is inherently bad; and still others tout the virtues of full spectrum. And you know what? They're all right and at the same time all wrong. If there actually was one single absolute without a doubt works in all situations and conditions best way, everyone would be doing it, and there would be no arguments. What you use at a particular time and location is entirely situational based on a myriad of factors including but not limited to: environmental conditions (dusty, raining, freezing, flying insects, etc.), lighting conditions (total darkness, partial or full lighting, natural or artificial), indoor or outdoor location, distances, reflective surfaces, etc. etc. etc. etc.

Again, that's where knowing the capabilities and limitations of your equipment, including your still and video cameras, are paramount to your success. I can't teach you this by simply describing it. You have to do that yourself thru actual hands-on practice. Since this is not a book on general photography, I don't think it would be helpful or even cogent for me to attempt to explain things like shutter speeds, depth of field, or aperture in this limited venue. I defer to the real experts on this matter. I'm also not going to get into a long winded discussion on Orbs (which has been discussed and debated forever with no conclusion), film versus digital (virtually no one uses film anymore), or anything else that you absolutely need to experience first-hand. Some of you may look at this as a copout, but so be it.

Leading you through the process in person is one thing, trying to teach, or even explain rudimentarily, something that is primarily a personal hands-on learning experience by way of a few paragraphs or pages is another. With today's digital cameras, even the lower priced ones; you have all the controls and mechanical capabilities you need at hand to be successful, if you'll simply apply yourself. Once you then reach a point where you're comfortable and proficient with what you have, you can move on to the next step. Explore new or different technologies, learn new processes and strategies, experiment, and develop your own skills and abilities.

Start taking photographs and video and you'll quickly find yourself hooked. You'll become like an addict searching for a fix, or in this case searching for that positive affirmation; by actually catching a still picture or video that will then in turn validate your beliefs and make all the hard work and long hours' worth it. A psychological high as it were. I will admit that I'm a recovering addict when it comes to ghost photography. I say recovering because even though I am addicted, I've learned to curb that overwhelming need to compulsively micro examine everything and see things that are really not there. It took me a awhile to realize that my extreme psychological need to see something paranormal in every photo was actually a detriment to the entire process. The same thing is also applicable to EVP's too. It's hard to explain, but you have to take on, to a degree, the role of the skeptic and assume there is nothing there to begin with. Once you take on that mindset, any actual anomalies in a photograph or video will instantly stand out or at least be more readily discernable.

To finalize this section, I'll leave you with a few universal common sense suggestions, comments, and tips to think about and remember when out investigating.

(1) Always be courteous, announce your intentions, and/or ask permission prior to taking photographs of people, private places, AND spirits.
(2) Leave everything as you originally found it, period!
(3) If you are taking pictures in cemeteries, battlefields, churches – show reverence and respect!
(4) Keep your camera still to avoid blurry photographs. Duh.
(5) Take lots and lots of pictures, way more than you think you need. Remember, when you shoot digitally

you're not incurring any extra cost, except the time to evaluate them all.

(6) Keep your camera lens clean at all times. Again Duh.

(7) Make sure to keep camera strap, lens cap, and stray hair tied back and out of the picture.

(8) Avoid pointing your camera at direct light sources to avoid lens flare.

(9) Watch your breath in extremely cold weather.

(10) Occasionally take a picture over your shoulder (you just might be being followed by a ghost).

(11) Beware reflective surfaces, especially when using flash.

(12) Blowing dust, insects, fog, and rain can cause false anomalies such as mists, light streaks, and orbs.

(13) Don't smoke in any area that's going to be photographed.

(14) Always try to take two or three pictures in the same location for comparison purposes.

Note: Ghost photography is not strictly a nighttime activity, done in complete darkness. In fact, the majority of the most compelling and famous ghost or spirit photographs ever taken were either during the day or under fairly well lit conditions.

Keep in mind that there are no "best" places to photograph. While there are some locations that may have a higher propensity for ghostly activity and with it a larger number of past captures; ghosts, like people, can be anywhere at any time. You may want to focus your activity in the known hotspots areas, but don't rule out any location. Go with that gut feeling and keep that camera handy.

My suggestion is that you take your camera out and practice with it in every kind of condition you can think of, apart from any ghost hunting; complete darkness, normal lighting, daytime, dusty, freezing, inside with and without reflective surfaces, with and without flash, etc. to make sure you're entirely familiar with the process and results that should be expected in those different conditions.

Psychics, Dogs/Cats, Dowsing Rods, and Spirit Boards

The common denominator here is "sensitivity" - Sensitivity to the spirit world in a direct manner (i.e. psychic mediums and animals, particularly dogs and cats) and by way of some amplification or drawing in procedure (i.e. dowsing rods/pendulums and spirit (Ouija) boards). From my perspective, I love both psychic mediums and animals, am sort of ambivalent about dowsing rods and pendulums, and am absolutely against the use of spirit boards, especially in the hands of somebody who is untrained, inexperienced, and unaware of the consequences of potentially drawing in some type of negative entity. If you or one of your team members has the ability to use dowsing rods or a pendulum, by all means use them. I look at those devices more as a psychically powered detector of something already present, rather than a means of opening a pathway for potentially malevolent or evil spirits to come in, that you'll get way too often, with the spirit board.

The information you can garner from a psychic medium can be very valuable to any investigation.

They can help narrow the focus of your investigation, possibly identify who or what may be present, help determine why particular entities are there, validate your present research efforts, uncover new and previously unknown historical facts, and possibly even determine whether it's actually safe to proceed with an investigation.

There has been much argument among investigators as to how a psychic medium's services should be utilized in an investigation. Should they conduct a separate uncontaminated blind walkthrough prior to the investigation, much like you see in the television show Dead Files; or should they accompany you during the course of an entire investigation? In my mind there is really no right answer, so just go with whatever feels right for you at that time. If you do find yourself privileged to have a truly gifted psychic medium willing to participate in your investigation(s), thank your lucky stars.

When it comes to animals, they tend to react to the presence of spirits in many ways. Their particular type of reaction (i.e. scared, docile, or aggressive) may give you an indication as to what type of entity, passive or malevolent, you may be dealing with; and where it, or they, may be located at that point in time within the property. Know that not every animal has the temperament or disposition necessary to be a good ghost hunter, so don't push it. Keep in mind though; whether it's a psychic medium's descriptive feelings or rover's reactions, it's still just a piece of the puzzle and should be considered for what it is, just another investigative tool in your arsenal of many.

Protection before, during, and after the Investigation

One of the most important, and potentially more dangerous, aspects of dealing with the ghostly realm during an investigation is the potential for spirit attack and spirit attachment. I'm constantly amazed at how many investigators ignore or give only cursory acknowledgement to the potential dangers here. While not by any means an everyday occurrence, it does happen often enough for you to take heed, and to make sure you and your team members have put in place safeguards to minimize and hopefully eliminate the, at least, potential threat.

My own general definition of spirit attack would be: a malicious and purposeful physical or psychic attack, perpetrated by some unseen spirit or entity, which results in pain and/or injury. The key here is malicious and purposeful. Things such as: touching, light hair pulling, light pushing, or clothes' tugging is not spirit attack. Getting slammed up against the wall, pushed down stairs, severely scratched, or having a large solid object thrown at you would in my mind definitely constitute an attack. 99.9% of the time, spirits have absolutely no inclination to try and harm you in any way. They may in fact actually be scared of you. Pretty much any time that you get touched, they're simply trying to get your attention and to make you aware of their presence.

You will however, on that very rare occasion, run into the more malevolent acting spirit who may not like the living in general, may not like you in particular, may be protective of the location, or maybe just does not like to be disturbed and hassled in any way, and will lash out in hopes of getting you to leave. Another thing to always consider is, the very remote possibility that you may be dealing with some more nasty demonic type entity.

The simplest definition of spirit attachment is: an invasion of a human body by an unseen spirit or entity. Some people may refer to this as "jumping" or "getting jumped". The effects of spirit attachment can run the gamut from mild energy drain, extreme personality change, serious unexplained illness, and other nasty changes in both psychological and physical condition. The effects can be both temporary and long-term. Speculation as to the reason why this may occur varies from the spirit or entity being simply attracted to a person's life energy to a purposeful takeover of the human body for nefarious purposes. Much of this can be directly attributed to the physical health and mental condition of the investigator at the time an attack or attachment occurs. In other words, if you are physically and mentally healthy, radiate positive energy, and are not angry, grief stricken, fearful, anxious, or under the influence of drugs or alcohol then you can usually stave off most problems. Negative spirits and entities are attracted to the physically and emotionally weak. That's one of the reasons why you never want to investigate when you're not feeling well or are carrying a lot of emotional baggage.

As I said; your best initial defense is to always maintain yourself at peak physical and emotional condition while investigating. There are also a number of other simple and easy methods that can be utilized to help create a more impregnable wall or shield against these potential aggressive incursions, if you'll just learn to use them.

(1) Prayer

A simple prayer asking for protection, done individually or as a group, is very effective. This should be done at the very beginning of the investigation and again anytime you leave the location for any extended period of time. At the end of an investigation I would also recommend that you do an additional "thank you" protection prayer that would also include telling all spirits and entities they are not allowed to follow you home. It really doesn't make any difference what the exact wordings of your prayers are, as long as it is from the heart.

(2) White Light Visualization

This can also be done individually, or as a group. Close your eyes and visualize a beam of pure white light coming down from the heavens (imagine standing in bright sunlight), enveloping your entire body. Now visualize that pure white light entering your body and pushing out and extinguishing all negativity within you. Then further extend it maybe 6 to 12 inches beyond you to form a shield that will effectively repel any negative influences. This can be repeated again at any time you feel threatened or uneasy during an investigation. I've found it particularly effective to do this in conjunction with a prayer of protection.

(3) Amulets and Religious Symbols

An amulet (Latin amuletum) is an object with alleged power to protect its owner from danger or harm. This would generally include gems, especially engraved gems, statues, coins, drawings, pendants, and rings. Religious symbols such as the Christian Cross, the Pentagram (Seal of Solomon), and Hexagram (Star of David) would also be included here.

What you choose, or rather what chooses you; is individualized according to need and personal preference. I can tell you from my own personal experience that I've never really felt anything from crystals or gemstones. Many people do, but then again that goes back to individualization. My personal preference is a custom one; a Pentagram overlaid by a small Christian Cross which I wear around my neck or keep in my pocket. Whatever you may use, just remember to cleanse it, consecrate it, and charge it with your own positive personal energy periodically.

There could be a situation that would require an even more aggressive response, namely banishment. You may command a spirit or entity to depart using the words "the power of God compels you", call upon your Guardian Angel to assist, or call upon the Archangel Michael; which I've personally found to be particularly effective. If you've done your duty from the beginning in reassuring any spirits or entities present that you mean them no harm and are only looking for answers and despite this, receive some injurious response, then you have to respond in kind. A zero tolerance policy, if you will.

Remember, your protection and/or banishment actions are not aimed at the good spirits, only the malevolent ones. There are other procedures and processes you can employ such as smudging, salt barriers, holy water, house blessing, and up to and including exorcism depending on need and severity. If in doubt, don't hesitate to call in an experienced professional for help.

Never an End – Only a Beginning

To reiterate: "Paranormal investigation in general, by its very nature and subject matter, does not operate in or conform to the rigid set of hierarchical scientific rules, designed for the physical world alone. Sometimes things happen that simply defy logic and fail to conform to what we normally perceive and believe as possible. Because we have yet to conclusively prove something, does not mean it doesn't in fact exist. The paranormal investigator is one who realizes that and yet still continues their quest, in spite of any adversity. To the TRUE paranormal investigator, "scientifically impossible" is simply something the scientific community utters and clings to when they themselves have thrown up their hands and given up".

We now come to the conclusion of the book, which hopefully is just the beginning of your journey into paranormal investigation. In writing this book my goal was not to be the definitive encyclopedia of everything pertaining to ghost hunting, or just something filled with lurid and exciting tales of haunted places and ghostly apparitions. Rather, I wanted to take a more basic, and hopefully more thought-provoking, approach to ghost hunting that could actually help set you on the right path to eventually becoming a great investigator. Always keep in mind that your number one job, as a paranormal investigator, is to gather compelling evidence of the existence of, in this case, ghosts and spirits. To do that you must be a believer and a skeptic at the same time; logical, adaptable, observant, intuitive, and creative.

Above all else you need to feel the joy, excitement, and thrill of the hunt that we all get; each and every time you go out. If you have that and lose it, it becomes simply a job that pays nothing. If you never feel that overwhelming desire to be an explorer, just stick with the guided tours. I for one prefer to be the explorer, to take chances, look for possibilities, and try to gather answers to the, so far, unknown and unexplained. Take what you may have learned here and expand on it. Read other books, join a group, experiment, and work on developing your own style and methods. Don't be a mere observer, be a participant.

Resources

Ghost Hunting Classes and Training

Ghost Hunter's Shop

http://www.ghosthuntershop.com

The Ghost Research Home Study Course

https://www.prairieghosts.com/ghost_course.html

Ghost Hunting Group Listings (US & International)

Paranormal Societies

http://www.paranormalsocieties.com/

GhostStop

http://www.ghoststop.com/ghost-hunting-teams-a/250.htm

Equipment Suppliers

GhostStop

Saint Cloud, FL

http://www.ghoststop.com

Ghost Hunter Store

Burlington, NJ

http://theghosthunterstore.com/

Ghost Hunters Equipment

St. Augustine, FL

http://www.ghosthuntersequipment.com

Ghost Hunter's Shop

Lexington, KY

http://www.ghosthuntershop.com

Haunted Locations that you may want to visit

The West Virginia State Penitentiary is located in Moundsville and operated from 1876 to 1995. It was ranked as one of the United States Department of Justice's Top Ten Most Violent Correctional Facilities. From 1899 to 1959, ninety-four men were executed. In total, 36 known homicides took place in the prison. The prison was closed by court order on March 27, 1995 after it was determined by the court that the small 5x7 cells were too small and the living conditions were inhumane.

The Myrtles Plantation located in St. Francisville, Louisiana; is regarded by most as one of "America's Most Haunted Homes". Built by General David Bradford in 1796 it is on the National Register of Historic Places. Operated now as a Bed and Breakfast, they also give tours of the home and property. Said to be the home of at least 12 different ghosts.

The Waverly Hills Sanatorium in southwestern Louisville/Jefferson County, Kentucky was solely dedicated to the treatment of tuberculosis patients. The sanatorium operated from 1910 until 1962. Considered one of the "most haunted hospitals" in the eastern United States, it is estimated that as many as 63,000 people died there.

The Trans-Allegheny Lunatic Asylum, subsequently the Weston State Hospital, operated from 1864 until 1994 by the government of the state of West Virginia, in the city of Weston. It's considered to be one of the most haunted locations in America. Originally designed to hold 250 people, its patient population swelled starting in the 1950's to as many as 2400. It was forcibly closed in 1994 after years of what became to be considered barbaric patient treatment and abuse which included forced lobotomies. Thousands of patients died at the facility and some are even buried on the grounds of the property.

In 2005, Life Magazine called it "the most haunted house in America." Located in San Diego, CA the Whaley House was built in 1857 by Thomas Whaley and not only served as the Whaley family residence, but also at varying times as San Diego's first commercial theater, the county courthouse, and the Whaley and Crosthwaite General Store. The house is a California Historic Landmark and is listed by the United States Department of Commerce as an authentic haunted house.

Stull Cemetery located between Topeka and Kansas City, in the unincorporated town of Stull, Kansas, is listed by many haunting guides as not only one of the most haunted cemeteries in America, but one of the Seven Portals to Hell. The old church is now a pile of rubble. For years, stories and legends of witchcraft, ghosts, and supernatural happenings have surrounded the old graveyard. Beware, human trespassers may be prosecuted.

Lizzie Borden House was the site of one of the most
infamous crimes of all time, the murders of Andrew and
Abby Borden, reportedly at the hands of Andrew's
daughter Lizzie. As the nursery rhyme goes, "Lizzie
Borden took an axe and gave her mother forty whacks,
when she saw what she had done she gave her father
forty-one. Lizzie was charged with both murders but
eventually acquitted. No one else was charged in the
murders, and they continue to be the subject of research
and speculation, even today. The home of the murders still
stands in Fall River, MA and operates today as a bed-and-
breakfast.

Built in 1858 and located literally next door to the Alamo, the Menger Hotel holds the unofficial title of "The Most Haunted Hotel in Texas", claiming to host 32 different spirits including Sallie White, a maid who was murdered by her husband and buried at the hotel's expense. Notable past guests have included Ulysses S. Grant, Theodore Roosevelt Robert E. Lee, Dwight D. Eisenhower, Mae West, Babe Ruth, Oscar Wilde, Lillie Langtry, Cornelius Vanderbilt, and William McKinley to name a few.

The Stanley Hotel is a 140-room neo-Georgian hotel in Estes Park, Colorado located within sight of the Rocky Mountain National Park. It was built by Freelan Oscar Stanley of Stanley Steamer fame and opened on July 4, 1909. The Stanley is best known as the inspiration for Stephen King's novel "The Shining". The hotel is allegedly haunted by at least twelve ghosts, including that of the founder, Freelan O. Stanley. From all accounts it appears that the spirits that seem to linger in and around the hotel have no malicious intent and simply enjoy the location, much as the living visitors do.

The McPike Mansion built in 1869 for the McPike family. The Italianate-Victorian style home featured 16 rooms, 11 marble fireplaces, beautifully carved stairway banisters and a vaulted wine cellar.. After 1950 the property sat abandoned and was heavily damaged by both the weather and vandals until new owners purchased it in 1994. This house is considered the most haunted location in Alton, IL as well as one of the most haunted houses in North America. The apparitions of former occupants are seen both in the house and on the grounds. All proceeds of McPike Mansion tours and functions go towards restoration of this Historic Site.

Founded in 1859, the old gold mining town of Bodie is considered to be California's most famous and best preserved, as well as the nation's largest unreconstructed ghost town (200 buildings). Bodie is a National Historic Landmark and a State Historic Park. It receives about 200,000 visitors yearly. The Bodie Curse - If someone removes any object from the town they are doomed to misfortune until they return that which they have taken. Park officials receive countless items back each year after those individuals' responsible have experienced both tragic events and unexplainable bad luck.

Glossary of Paranormal Terms

Afterlife

Life after our physical body dies.

Akashic Records

The akashic records is a term used in Theosophy to describe a compendium of mystical knowledge encoded in a non-physical plane of existence.

Alchemy

Is both a philosophy and an ancient practice focused on the attempt to change base metals into gold, investigating the preparation of the "elixir of longevity", and achieving ultimate wisdom.

Amorphous

Having no definite form or shape. Spirits and ghosts often appear in mist-like forms or shapes.

Amulet

A symbol or object with magical significance which is worn as a pendant or ring to repel evil or bad luck.

Angel

An angel is considered a messenger of God. A celestial being that is benevolent in nature, possesses miraculous abilities and whose role includes protecting and guiding human beings.

Animism

The belief that souls or spirits exist not only in humans but also in animals and the natural environment.

Anomaly

An anomaly is any occurrence or object that is strange, unusual, or unique.

Apparition

An unusual, unexplainable, and sudden appearance.

Apport

The arrival or materialization of an object during a haunting, these can be animate or inanimate.

Asport

The disappearance, or dematerialization, of objects that will then reappear elsewhere.

Astral Travel

Theory that a person's spiritual awareness can temporarily detach itself from the physical body and travel to and experience things in other locations, time frames or dimensional planes.

Aura

An aura is a field of subtle, luminous energy radiating from and surrounding a person or object.

Automatic Writing

Phenomena by which people write without conscious thought.

Automatism

A process in which the subconscious communicates with the conscious by means of a vehicle such as a Ouija Board, automatic writing, or pendulum swinging.

Banishing

Formal, ceremonial, procedure used to cast a spirit or entity out from an area.

Banshee

A death omen in Irish folklore that manifests in wailing screams to herald an upcoming death.

Benign Spirit

A spirit that is not harmful.

Bibliomancy

The practice of divination by randomly selecting a page in the Bible.

Bilocation

Appearing to be in two different places at the same time.

Boogey Man

A grim spectral figure that delights in menacing the living.

Calling Ghosts

These are ghosts that call out the name of the living in order to get their attention.

Channeling

The process that some mediums use for communication with the deceased.

Clairvoyant

Someone with the psychic ability to see events or people which have not occurred yet.

Clairaudient

The psychic ability to hear voices and sounds inaudible to the normal human ear.

Cleansing

The act of performing a formal and ritualistic purification of an area. Prayers, religious rites, special artifacts, incantations, and various herbs or liquids (such as holy water) are used in such rituals with the purpose of either ridding the area of an existing entity, or preventing entities from entering the area.

Cold Spot

An area where the temperature is lower than the surrounding environment. Cold spots are believed to be created when a ghost is presence within that area.

Collective Apparition

An apparition seen by several people at the same time.

Crisis Apparition

An apparition that is seen when a person is seriously ill, seriously injured or at the point of death.

Crossroads

Crossroads are said to be haunted by various entities who lead confused travelers astray.

Cryptozoology

Cryptozoology refers to the search for animals which are considered to be legendary or otherwise nonexistent by mainstream biology.

Curse

An appeal or prayer for evil or misfortune to befall someone or something as well as the after effect on the desired target.

Deja`Vu

A person's feeling that current events have been experienced before.

Deep Trace Medium

A psychic who allows a spirit to enter their body so that the spirits can communicate through them.

Dematerialization

The fading or disappearance of a physical object.

Demon

A hostile and aggressive spirit without human origin. In religious terms, it is seen as evil and associated with the Devil.

Devil

The Devil is a title given to the supernatural entity, who, in Christianity, Islam, and other religions, is a powerful, evil entity and the tempter of humankind. The Devil commands a force of lesser evil spirits, commonly known as demons.

Disembodied

A spirit that is functioning without a physical body.

Disembodied Voice

A voice emanating from no known source.

Divination

Obtaining knowledge of future events by the use of outside psychic or spirit forces.

Doppelganger

A doppelgänger is a ghostly double of a living person, often perceived as a sinister form of bilocation.

Dowser

A dowser is a psychic with radiesthetic sense who

can detect animate and inanimate objects by using dowsing rods or a pendulum.

Dowsing Rod

A bent or v shaped rod sometimes made from a forked tree branch, coat hanger, or welding rod.

Dynamic EM Field

A changing electromagnetic field often associated with a nearby power line or radio source.

Earthbound

A term referring to a ghost or spirit that was unable to cross over to the other side at the time of death and is therefore stuck on earth.

Ectoplasm

A term coined by Charles Richet to denote a substance or spiritual energy "exteriorized" by physical mediums, associated with the formation of ghosts, and asserted to be an enabling factor in psychokinesis.

Electromagnetic Field (EMF)

A magnetic energy field that radiates from an energy source such as lights, appliances, transformers, ac wiring, and even the earth itself.

Electronic Voice Phenomena (EVP)

The recording of noises (voices) which are out of the range of human hearing.

Elementals

In magical tradition and ceremony, spirits which govern the four corners of the earth and are associated with, or reside within, the four basic elements.

EMF Detector

An EMF detector is a device that measures and detects changes in an electromagnetic field.

Empathy

Sensitive to the feelings, emotions, thoughts, and experience of another, past or present.

Entity

A being or bodiless form of existence, most commonly referred to as ghost or spirit.

Evocation

The summoning of spirits by usage of ritual, gesture, or verse of incantation.

Exorcism

The ritualistic and religious purging of a spirit from a person or place.

Extrasensory Perception

A person's ability to gain information about people, places, or events which cannot be gained by simply using one's normal five senses.

Faraday Cage

A shield used to block an EM Field from interacting with whatever is enclosed in the cage.

Fortean Event

Named for Charles Fort, it has become a catch all term for paranormal events of all kinds.

Gauss Meter

A device that is used to measure the electromagnetic field, also referred to as an EMF detectors or a magnetometer.

Ghost

According to traditional belief, a ghost is the soul or spirit of a deceased person, taken to be capable of appearing in visible form or otherwise manifesting itself to the living.

Ghost Building

The appearance of a building or part of a building that no longer exists.

Ghost Lights

Unexplainable lights that are large and bright in appearance.

Ghost Ship

The appearance of a ship that has been known to have wrecked or disappeared years or centuries before.

God

The name God refers to the deity held by monotheists to be the supreme reality. God is generally regarded as the sole creator of the universe. Theologians have ascribed certain attributes to God, including omniscience, omnipotence, omnipresence, perfect goodness, divine simplicity, and eternal and necessary existence.

Guardian Spirit (Guardian Angel)

A guardian angel is a spirit who protects and guides a particular person.

Haunted

A person, place or an object to which a spirit is attached.

Haunting

The presence of an entity or entities associated with one or more persons, places, or objects.

Heaven

Heaven is a plane of existence in religions and spiritual philosophies, typically described as the holiest possible place, accessible by people according to various standards of divinity (goodness, piety, etc.) Christians generally hold that it is the afterlife destination of those who have accepted Jesus Christ as their savior.

Hell

Hell, according to many religious beliefs, is an afterlife of suffering where the wicked or unrighteous dead are punished. Hells are almost always depicted as underground. Christianity and Islam traditionally depict hell as fiery, Hells from other traditions, however, are sometimes cold and gloomy. Alternatively, Hell would not be a place or locality but a state of being, where one is separated from God - thought to be held back by un-repented sin and/or corruption of spirit.

Hex

A negative magical working, or spell, cast to influence a person's will or fate.

Hyperesthesia

An extraordinarily and acute sensory awareness.

Icon

A rendering or image of a particular person or scene, with religious significance.

Imp

A nature spirit who does more harm than good.

Incubus

A demon in male form supposed to seduce and/or sexually assault females. Its female counterpart is the succubus.

Infestation

Repeated and persistent paranormal phenomena, generally centered on a particular location or person.

Intelligent haunting

A haunting in which a spiritual entity is aware of the living world and interacts with or responds to it.

Intuition

To know or sense something without having any prior knowledge.

Invocation

The summoning of spirits.

Jinx

A period of bad luck thought to be brought on by a spell.

Karma

The effect on and result of, a person's actions and conduct during the successive phases of the person's existence, commonly referred to as cause and effect.

Kirlian photography

A technique for photographing spiritual auras.

Lepke

A ghost which has the appearance of a solid, living person, may even converse with someone, then suddenly vanish.

Lens flare

The light scattering effect that occurs in the lens system of a camera.

Ley lines

Invisible lines of the earth's energy which align sacred sites such as churches and burial grounds. The area on which a ley line crosses is said to be a powerful point for paranormal activity.

Light Trance Medium

A person whom spirits can communicate through without going into a deep trance state.

Lore

All the facts and traditions about a particular subject

that have been accumulated over time through education or experience.

Magic

Sometimes known as sorcery, is the practice of consciousness manipulation and/or autosuggestion to achieve a desired result, usually by techniques described in various conceptual systems.

Magnetometer (EMF detector, gauss meter)

A device to measure the presence of a magnetic field, as well as its strength, direction, and fluctuation.

Malevolent Spirit

A malevolent spirit is one that wishes to do harm.

Malicious Spirit

These spirits will destroy or damage things of a personal or financial value for the sake of hurting others.

Manifestation

The appearance or taking form of an entity.

Materialization

The sudden appearance of something with little or no explanation as to the origin.

Matrixing

Finding recognizable (faces) shapes in inanimate objects or photographs where there no shape exists.

Medium

A person that acts as a bridge between the living and the dead.

Metaphysics

The line of philosophical thought which seeks knowledge beyond the laws of physics. It is concerned with explaining the fundamental nature of being and the world.

Near-Death Experience (NDE)

Experiences of people after they have been pronounced clinically dead, or been very close to death.

Necromancy

A form of magic in which the practitioner seeks to summon the spirit of a deceased person, either as an apparition or ghost, or to raise them bodily, for the purpose of divination.

Nexus

The transitional, or joining point connecting physical matter and pure energy,

Numerology

The study of numbers in regard to a person's character and life plan.

Obsession

The second stage of a haunting where a spirit dominates the mind of a living person.

Occam's Razor

The principle that we should always prefer the simplest explanation of events.

Occultism

Esoteric systems of belief and practice that assume the existence of mysterious forces and entities.

Oracle

A person or agency considered to be a source of wise counsel or prophetic opinion.

Orb

Name given to typically circular anomalies appearing in photographs. In photography and video, orbs appear to be balls, diamonds, or smears of light with an apparent size in the image ranging from a golf ball to a basketball. Orbs sometimes appear to be in motion, leaving a trail behind them.

Ouija Board

A spirit board or talking board, is a flat board marked with letters, numbers, and other symbols, supposedly used to communicate with spirits.

Outward Manifestation

The physical manifestation of paranormal activity.

Paranormal

Experiences that lie outside the range of normal experience or scientific explanation, or that indicates phenomena that is understood to be outside of science's current ability to explain or measure.

Parapsychology

A discipline that seeks to investigate the existence and causes of psychic abilities and life after death using scientific methods.

Pareidolia/Matrixing

Describes a psychological phenomenon involving a vague and random stimulus being perceived as significant. The mind's need to relate to an unfamiliar noise or image by creating a familiar one. Example: Seeing faces/objects in photographs that don't actually exist.

Phantom

An apparition or a spectre.

Phantomania

Paralysis that occurs when someone is under attack from some supernatural force; also known as psychic paralysis.

Phenomena

Any occurrence that is observable

Poltergeist

Meaning "noisy ghost"; is an entity that manifests itself by creating noise or moving objects. The phenomenon is believed to be caused by a specific individual or agent, frequently a child or adolescent.

Possession

The condition or affliction of being psychically or physically possessed by a demon or other supernatural entity.

Precognition

Also called future sight refers to perception that involves the acquisition of future information that cannot be deduced from presently available and normally acquired sense-based information.

Premonition

Feeling or warning about future events.

Preternatural

Associated with inhuman, demonic or diabolical spirits or forces.

Psychic

A person who professes an ability to perceive

information hidden from the normal senses through extrasensory perception.

Psychic Cleansing

A less ritualized form of exorcism, wherein a site is purified and malevolent influences banished through prayers, which are spoken as the petitioner moves through the area.

Psychic Vampire

This is a term for individuals who seem to instinctively draw and absorb the psychic energies from others.

Psychokinesis (telekinesis)

The terms psychokinesis and telekinesis refer to the ability to exert physical force or move objects with only the mind.

Psychometry

The ability to sense information from an object, or from the surrounding environment.

Quantum Mechanics

Quantum mechanics is the study of the relationship between energy and matter.

Radio voice phenomenon (RVP)

Receiving the voice of a spirit over a regular radio.

Reincarnation

The belief that a person's soul will, following bodily

death, inhabit a new body in a long cycle of rebirths, purportedly for the soul's evolution through gaining experience.

Remote viewing

The claimed ability of an individual to view a location at a long distance.

Residual Haunting

Residual hauntings are repeated playbacks of auditory, visual, olfactory, and other sensory phenomena that are attributed to a traumatic event, life-altering event, or a routine event of a person or place, like an echo or a replay of a videotape of past events.

Retrocognition

The psychic perception of past events or conditions.

Séance

A séance is an attempt to communicate with spirits.

Shaman

A tribal priest who uses the forces of magic to effect healings and divinations.

Shape shifter

Entity with the ability to assume the form of another person, an animal or other entity.

Singularity

An event which is completely rare and unique, and cannot be scientifically explained.

Skeptic

Someone who habitually doubts accepted beliefs, One who is yet undecided as to what is true; one who is looking or inquiring for what is true or an inquirer after facts or reasons.

Skeptical

Of or pertaining to a skeptic or skepticism; characterized by skepticism; hesitating to admit the certainty of doctrines or principles; doubting of everything.

Sleep Paralysis

A state of seeming to be awake but unable to move.

Spectre

A ghost or apparition.

Spirit

A non-corporeal substance contrasted with the material body.

Spirit photography

The art or process of taking photographs to capture images of spirits.

Spirit Rescue

Attempting contact with entities, intended to alleviate the entities' distress and aid them in the resolution of their conflicts or to cross over to a higher, spiritual plane.

Spiritualist

One who believes in the communication between this world and the invisible world.

Stigmata

Bodily marks, sores, or sensations of pain in locations corresponding to the crucifixion wounds of Jesus.

Subliminal Perception

Perceiving without conscious awareness.

Succubus

A female demonic creature who seduces men in their sleep. Its male counterpart is the incubus.

Superstition

The unfounded belief that certain objects, activities or rituals can be either helpful or harmful.

Synchronicity

The experience of two or more events, which are apparently causally unrelated, occurring together in a meaningful manner.

Talisman

A design or inscription that is worn, carried or displayed, for the purpose of invoking strength, power, protection or the aid of spirits.

Telekinesis (psychokinesis)

The terms psychokinesis and telekinesis refer to the ability to exert physical force or move objects with only the mind.

Telepathy

The ability to communicate directly through mind-to-mind contact.

Thought Transference

The telepathic transmission of images and messages from the mind of one person to that of another.

Time-displacement

The experience of a time span separate from the actual time span of the observer.

Ufology

The study of UFOs.

Printed in Great Britain
by Amazon

12630989R00093